Canaries Reflect on the Mine

Dropouts' Stories of Schooling

A volume in
Research for Social Justice: Personal~Passionate~Participatory Inquiry
Ming Fang He and JoAnn Phillion, *Series Editors*

Canaries Reflect on the Mine

Dropouts' Stories of Schooling

Jeanne Cameron
Tompkins Cortland Community College

INFORMATION AGE PUBLISHING, INC.
Charlotte, NC • www.infoagepub.com

Library of Congress Cataloging-in-Publication Data

Cameron, Jeanne.
 Canaries reflect on the mine : dropouts' stories of schooling / Jeanne
Cameron.
     p. cm. – (Research for social justice: personal, passionate,
participatory inquiry)
 Includes bibliographical references.
 ISBN 978-1-61735-998-9 (pbk.) – ISBN 978-1-61735-999-6 (hardcover) –
ISBN 978-1-62396-000-1 (ebook) 1. High school dropouts–United
States–Case studies. I. Title.
 LC146.5.C36 2012
 373.12'913–dc23

                                                    2012025481

Printed in the United States of America

Contents

Acknowledgements vii

Series Foreword: Research for Social Justice:
Personal~Passionate~Participatory Inquiry ix
   Ming Fang He and JoAnn Phillion

Foreword xv
   William H. Schubert

Prologue xix

1   Narrative Research and Sociological Poetry 1

2   Hannah: Pushing Back, Moving On 17

3   Steve: A Gambler's Story 25

4   Adel: Refusing to be Left Behind 37

5   Cole: Making Money, Making Sense 47

6   Isabel: "I pretty much felt like I wasn't even there" 53

7   Iris: A Voice not Heard 61

8   Ivan: Loss of Faith 69

9   Canaries in the Mine 83

10 Spin and Whisper 105

   References 119

   Notes 127

Acknowledgements

From my remarkable mother, Wilma Page McPherson, I learned to look for the good in people and to be generous with the benefit of the doubt. From my brilliant and iconoclastic social theory professor, Frank Hearn, I learned to look at the larger world through a lens inspired by C. Wright Mills. Wilma and Frank, two working class heroes, fostered the particular disposition I needed to do this work well. Their gifts have also made me a richer person in all of the ways that really count.

For 25 years, my husband John has shared stories of hope and wonder that are authored each day in his urban classroom. The systematic assault on the work of good teachers, advanced by No Child Left Behind and Race to the Top, has pierced his spirit but has not diminished the reverence he has for his young students and their families. He is a daily reminder of the tremendous power teachers have to do good when they care deeply, know their students fully, and refuse to comply with "reforms" that hurt children, even when doing so comes at a great personal cost.

My children, Nick and Paige, have schooled me daily on how to *see* and *hear* children and youth. When I have been a slow learner, they have been patient, but insistent. I could not have heard the young people I worked with on this project so clearly or so well without the benefit of my children's lessons. A special thanks goes to Paige for carefully reading the full manuscript, for letting Isabel break her heart, and for saying, "I didn't expect the prose to be so pretty, mom. You have some [Markus] Zusak moments."

Canaries Reflect on the Mine, pages vii–viii
Copyright © 2012 by Information Age Publishing

Special thanks go to my colleagues and administrators at Tompkins Cortland Community College for supporting my sabbatical to conduct this research; to Ces Scott for her enthusiasm for this project and for being an endless source of information and support; to Caroline McKenzie for her close reading of the final manuscript; and to my dear friends John Marciano, Rochelle Mike, Phil Tate, Darlene Gold, and Karen Pastorello, for reading countless versions of individual chapters, for making insightful recommendations, and for cheering me on. Thanks also to John Sinsabaugh, the talented young artist who designed the book's cover.

Thanks to Chris Liska Carger (2009) for writing *Dreams Deferred: Dropping Out and Struggling Forward*. Her powerful story of Alejandro and his family introduced me to this special book series. An especially warm thank you goes to Ming Fang He and JoAnn Phillion for crafting a series that is unapologetically committed to social justice and to inquiry that is personal, passionate, and participatory. They have created a much needed home for books like *Canaries Reflect on the Mine*. Thanks also to George F. Johnson, publisher and president of Information Age Publishing, for seeing the value in such a series. A very warm thank you as well goes to William Schubert, for kindly agreeing to read *Canaries* and for writing a foreword that so clearly recognizes and affirms the wisdom of the young people who brought this book to life.

The biggest shout out, of course, goes to the young people who have storied these pages. Thank you for your generosity, your bravery, your wisdom, your tenacity, and your grace. Thank you for your fierce hope that your stories will make a difference in the lives of other young people coming up through our public school system. Thank you for exploding the stereotypes that are used to dismiss you. Thank you for bodying the "statistics" that numb us. Thank you for lifting our anesthetic veil.

Series Foreword

Research for Social Justice: Personal~Passionate~Participatory Inquiry

Ming Fang He and JoAnn Phillion

esearch for Social Justice: Personal~Passionate~Participatory Inquiry is a book series that features social justice research on life in schools, families, and communities. This work connects the personal with the political, the theoretical with the practical, and research with social and educational change. The inquiries demonstrate three distinct and interconnected qualities. Each is personal, compelled by values and experiences researchers bring to the work. Each is passionate, grounded in a commitment to social justice concerns of people and places under consideration. Each is participatory, built on long-term, heart-felt engagement, and shared efforts. The principal aspects of the inquiries that distinguish them from others are that researchers are not detached observers, nor putatively objective recorders, but active participants in schools, families, and communities. Researchers engaged in this form of inquiry have explicit research agendas that focus on equity, equality, and social justice. Rather than aiming solely at traditional educational research outcomes, positive social and educational change is the focal outcome of inquiry.

Researchers engaged in personal~passionate~participatory inquiry in this series are diverse, and their inquiries are far ranging in terms of content, people, and geographic locations studied. Their studies reflect new

Canaries Reflect on the Mine, pages ix–xiii

and exciting ways of researching and representing experiences of disenfranchised, underrepresented, and invisible groups and challenge stereotypical or deficit perspectives on these groups. It is our hope that this book series will inspire pre-service and in-service teachers, educators, educational researchers, administrators, and educational policy makers to commit to the enactment of educational and social change that fosters equity, equality and social justice.

The work in this book series draws on diverse research traditions that promote social justice (Ayers, Quinn, & Stovall, 2008) and the *democratic ideal* (Dewey, 1916) in education and life. The work of Du Bois (1903/1994), Cooper (1892/1988), Woodson (1933/1977), Freire (1970), and Ayers (2006) has also influenced social justice work in terms of its emphasis on the emancipatory, participatory, and social activist aspects of research. This work builds upon narrative inquiry (Clandinin & Connelly, 2000; Schubert & Ayers, 1999), particularly cross-cultural and multicultural narrative inquiry (He, 2003; He & Phillion, 2008; Phillion, 2002; Phillion, He, & Connelly, 2005; Phillion & He, 2008) in response to recognition of the complexity of human experience in increasingly diversified societies. These researchers incorporate narrative, story, autobiography, memoir, fiction, oral history, documentary film, painting, and poetry into inquiries. One special quality of their inquiries that distinguishes them from other forms of educational research lies in understanding experience in its own terms rather than categorizing experience according to predetermined structures and theories (Phillion, 1999). Their inquiries are "peopled" with characters, rather than filled with categories and labels. In some forms of traditional educational research, experience is seen, shaped, and written about by the researcher using theoretically derived forms; in effect the experience is determined by the theory. Experience is the starting point of these inquiries and is in the forefront at every stage of research. Their inquiries arise from experiences of researchers and participants, rather than being formulated as abstract research questions, and they proceed by continual reference to experience as field texts are collected, analyzed, and interpreted, and as meanings are crafted.

Researchers engaged in this form of inquiry also draw on Critical Race Theory (Gutierrez-Jones, 2001; hooks, 1991; Ladson-Billings, 1998, 2003; Parker, Deyhle, & Villenas, 1999; Stovall, 2005) and use stories to disclose hidden and silenced narratives of suppressed and underrepresented groups to counter meta-narratives that portray these groups as deficient and inferior. They ask themselves questions about what is missing from the *official story* that will make the problems of the oppressed more understandable. By telling counter stories, researchers recognize the importance of commitment to equity and social justice and their obligation to link inquiry to social and educational change. The explicit aim of democratic and social justice work is to engage with oppressed groups and individuals and empower them to take effective action toward more just and humane conditions.

Three distinct and interconnected qualities, *personal~passionate~partic ipatory*, permeate the process of these social justice inquiries. Researchers not only collect, but often live in the stories of people with whom they engage in inquiry. They position stories collected in historical, socio-political, economic, linguistic, and cultural contexts, and contextualize their inquiries within struggles of under-represented individuals and groups. Stories are presented in life-like ways; readers vicariously experience complexities, contradictions and dilemmas of people's lives. There is a sense of "being there" and a sense of urgency for change. The stories told challenge orthodoxy, awaken critical consciousness, and create possibilities for change.

The work featured in this book series, embedded in life in schools, communities and societies on the one hand, and powerful ideas of being human with strong commitment to a just society on the other, is at the heart of social justice work. Researchers begin with conscious reflection on experience to challenge assumptions, "to raise embarrassing questions," and "to confront orthodoxy and dogma" (Ayers, 2006, p. 85). They listen to "issues that marginalized or disadvantaged people speak of with excitement, anger, fear, or hope . . ." (Ayers, 2006, p. 88). They learn directly from individuals and communities about problems and obstacles they face and explore possible solutions by drawing upon the experience and knowledge of participants. Researchers demonstrate strong commitment to the plight of their participants and the injustice embedded in the larger society. This commitment permeates every aspect of life, begins with small changes, and expands to larger contexts.

Personal~passionate~participatory inquiry thrives on the researcher's passionate involvement, strong commitment, and unfaltering advocacy for disenfranchised, underrepresented, and invisible individuals and groups. This passion, commitment, and advocacy can not be cultivated in isolation. Rather, it calls for researchers to work with allies in schools and communities, to take to heart the shared concerns of individuals and groups, to build a community to develop strategies for the enactment of educational and social change that fosters equity, equality, social justice, freedom, and human possibility. Such a community can only flourish when the efforts of researchers join with the efforts of all educational stakeholders—pre-service and in-service teachers, educators, administrators, educational policy makers, students, parents, and community members. We hope that the inquiries featured in this series will help social justice researchers and workers of this community move beyond boundaries, transgress orthodoxies, and build a participatory movement to promote a more balanced, fair, and equitable human condition. An expanded community such as this embodies possibilities and creates hope for more fulfilling, more equitable, more humane lives in an increasingly diversifying world.

References

Ayers, W. C. (2006). Trudge toward freedom: Educational research in the public interest. In G. Ladson-Billings & W. F. Tate (Eds.), *Education research in the public interest: Social justice, action and policy* (pp. 81–97). New York, NY: Teachers College Press.

Ayers, W. C., Quinn, T., & Stovall, D. (2008). *Handbook of social justice in education.* New York, NY: Routledge.

Clandinin, D. J. & Connelly, F. M. (2000). *Narrative inquiry.* San Francisco, CA: Jossey-Bass.

Cooper, A. (1988). *A voice form the South.* New York, NY: Oxford University Press. (Original work published 1892)

Dewey, J. (1916). *Democracy and education: An introduction to the philosophy of education.* New York, NY: Free Press.

Du Bois, W. E. B. (1994). *The souls of black folks.* New York, NY: Fine Creative Media. (Original work published 1903)

Freire, P. (1970). *A pedagogy of the oppressed.* New York, NY: Seabury.

Gutierrez-Jones, C. (2001). *Critical race narratives: A study of race, rhetoric, and injury.* New York, NY: New York University Press.

He, M. F. (2003). *A river forever flowing: Cross-cultural lives and identities in the multicultural landscape.* Greenwich, CT: Information Age Publishing.

He, M. F. & Phillion, J. (2008). *Personal~passionate~participatory inquiry into social justice in education.* Greenwich, CT: Information Age Publishing.

hooks, b. (1991). Narratives of struggle. In P. Mariani (Ed.), *Critical fictions: The politics of imaginative writing* (pp. 53–61). Seattle, WA: Bay.

Ladson-Billings, G. (1998). Just what is critical race theory and what's it doing in a nice field like education? *International Journal of Qualitative Studies in Education, 11*(1), 7–24.

Ladson-Billings, G. (Ed.). (2003). *Critical race theory perspectives on the social studies: The profession, policies, and curriculum.* Greenwich, CT: Information Age Publishing.

Parker, L., Deyhle, D., & Villenas, S. (1999). *Critical race theory and qualitative studies in education.* Boulder, CO: Westview.

Phillion, J. (1999). Narrative and formalistic approaches to the study of multiculturalism. *Curriculum Inquiry, 29*(1), 129–141.

Phillion, J. (2002). *Narrative inquiry in a multicultural landscape: Multicultural teaching and learning.* Westport, CT: Ablex.

Phillion, J. & He, M. F. (2008). Multicultural and cross-cultural narrative inquiry in educational research. *Thresholds in Education, 34*(1).

Phillion, J., He, M. F., & Connelly, F. M. (Eds.). (2005). *Narrative and experience in multicultural education.* Thousand Oaks, CA: Sage.

Schubert, W. H. & Ayers, W. C. (Eds.). (1999). *Teacher lore: Learning from our own experience.* Troy, NY: Educators International Press.

Stovall, D. (2005). A challenge to traditional theory: Critical race theory, African-American community organizers, and education. *Discourse: Studies in the Cultural Politics of Education, 26*(1), 95–108.

Woodson, C. G. (1977). *The mis-education of the Negro.* Trenton, NJ: Africa World Press. (Original work published 1933)

Foreword

William H. Schubert

I am so glad that you are reading the foreword of an amazing book, *Canaries Reflect on the Mine: Dropouts' Stories of Schooling*. It is one of the most powerful critiques of contemporary school reform I have read.

The canary metaphor in the title alludes to Singham's (1998) powerful image drawn from the practice of sending canaries into mines to check on the presence of carbon monoxide or methane gases. When the canaries stop singing, the mine is evacuated and repairs are made. However, when school "dropouts" stop singing, the academic and social methane remains. What can we learn from these canaries? What can we learn from "dropouts"?

Having learned about school life as a community college professor, spouse of an exemplary teacher, daughter of a remarkable mother, student of several excellent teachers, and mother of a son and daughter who brought her a wealth of understanding of life in schools, Jeanne Cameron, author of this book and an imaginative sociologist (Mills, 1959), brilliantly portrays lives of dropouts in rural schools. As you peruse the pages of this book, you will hear insightful critiques of schooling from those who have been pejoratively labeled "dropouts" by societies and schools, which have long been characterized as places of preparation for democracy, a sentiment that still oozes through the rhetoric of mission and vision statements, strategic plans, and myriad other policy and promotional documents for schools. The ways in which Cameron weaves the words of these former stu-

Canaries Reflect on the Mine, pages xv–xviii
Copyright © 2012 by Information Age Publishing
All rights of reproduction in any form reserved.

dents (now students of life on their own) to depict oppressive institutional structures and practices they face, and inimical policy mandates that *guide* them, make me realize that schooling is too often preparation for autocracy or oligarchy rather than for democracy. The heart-gripping stories of these "dropouts" yearning for hope for our schools to become seedbeds of democracy might be realized if we heed the warnings and recommendations of these canaries in our midst.

Jeanne Cameron begins by letting readers know who she is and why she is interested in dropouts. Reading her stories of schooling drawn from her teaching, parenting, and commitment to social justice reminds me of my own stories—my eight years as an elementary school teacher, my encounters with forces that called themselves *school reform,* and 36 years as a professor in the field of curriculum studies and teacher education. Her writing inspires my desire to write my own stories, and I bet it will do the same for you as you ponder her commentary and that of the former students with whom she interacts.

I am perplexed about what to call the thoughtful participants in Cameron's journey. It makes me reflect on the work of several of my former doctoral students. I think of Mark Perry's (2000) work at a Latino school that took *pushouts* from a large urban school district, Cynthia Robinson-Cole's (2007) stories of *pullouts* who felt compelled to leave school to support their loved ones—particularly by making money in prostitution—and Chris Carger's (1996, 2009) counter-stories of Alejandro, a Mexican-American young man who opts out of school because of his experience of repression and suppression and an urgency to make a living and to support his family. I refer to these as *optouts* (Schubert, 2009a). Whether we use the label *optouts, pullouts, pushouts,* or *dropouts,* the message is that all students need to be listened to and learned from as Brian Schultz (2010) so persuasively urges. Such listening is much more than a therapeutic gesture. Rather, it calls vibrantly for us to learn from those who are pushed out of schools and those who remain inside but feel outside.

Through the voices of the brilliant "dropouts" featured in this book and through the extraordinary commentary of Jeanne Cameron, we learn what seems obvious though is too seldom practiced in the lives of youths who come to our schools with the hope to learn and to thrive. They want to be known and valued. They yearn to create worthwhile purposes and to have the freedom to pursue such purposes. Time and again Cameron and her participants show and tell us of the importance of such a pursuit. Their yearning for being known, feeling valued, and being able to pursue meaningful purposes is not merely for a nice and self-fulfilling educational experience. It is absolutely necessary.

What, then, is the mysterious reason that these qualities, desired by everyone, are so rarely found in schooling? This is also part of my own inquiry (Schubert, 2009b) through Deweyan lenses for the dastardly opposition that prevents these simple truths from informing educational theory, policy, and practice. Dewey (1933) called it the *acquisitive society,* wherein everything meaningful is transformed into a commodity to be acquired. This acquisitiveness is built on greed, which Buddha identified as the primal cause of human suffering and Martha Nussbaum (2010) sees as a force of dehumanization.

Cameron writes perceptively of the *spin* and the *whisper* of educational reform, particularly in Chapter 10. I see her *spin* as the dominant and dominating force of greed, acquisitiveness, and abusive power that morphs and distorts meaning, goodness, and edification into test scores, diplomas, grade point averages, and obedient behavior. Cameron's *whisper* is the courageous and persistent voice of progressive educators who attempt to engage in meaningful relationships with their students in order to know them deeply, affirm their value, and realize their purposes. Cameron's whisper is also a great teaching that understands how purpose comes from pursuit of interest and a sense of relevance. This quest is ever evolving as *a river forever flowing* (He, 2003) that builds on long term and heart-felt democratic collaboration with an unfaltering commitment to "equity, equality, social justice, freedom, and human possibility" (He, 2010, p. 471; also see He & Phillion, 2008).

So, my reading of *Canaries Reflect on the Mine* augments my repertoire of practical examples of the need for policy and practice in education that provide more meaningful lives for all, rather than merely the competitive edge for globalized greed. This book is not a panacea; rather, there is much to overcome. Jeanne Cameron and her participants illuminate through this book that dropouts are everywhere—not only in urban and suburban areas, not only in small towns and rural communities, but also in schools sitting at the desks without meaning and purpose.

The big educational question as I see it, and as amplified by Jeanne Cameron and her collaborators, is blatantly this: Are educational policy makers, leaders, and schools as institutions capable of knowing individuals, valuing them, helping them create purpose, and providing them with the freedom and encouragement to strive for those purposes? I believe such educational experience is possible. How can we make it happen?

The stories in this book reveal that some teachers remarkably and surreptitiously finagle a moribund structure to create worthwhile educational experience despite the oppressiveness of NCLB, Race to the Top, and the plethora of testing within a façade of rigor (mortis?) that squelches *love, justice, and education* (Schubert, 2009b). This book sparks a fire that invigorates educators to take time to listen with compassion, to seek opportunities for purposeful learning, to overcome acquisitiveness with solidarity, to strive for love and justice, and to cultivate possibilities for a better world.

References

Carger, C. L. (1996). *Of borders and dreams: A Mexican American experience of urban education.* New York, NY: Teachers College Press.

Carger, C. L. (2009). *Dreams deferred: Dropping out and struggling forward.* Charlotte: NC: Information Age Publishing.

Dewey, J. (1933). Dewey outlines utopian schools. *New York Times,* April 23, E7.

He, M. F. (2003). *A river forever flowing: Cross-cultural lives and identities in the multicultural landscape.* Greenwich, CT: Information Age Publishing.

He, M. F. (2010). Exile pedagogy: Teaching and living in-between. In, J. A. Sandlin, B. D. Schultz, & J. Burdick (Eds.), *Handbook of public pedagogy: Education and learning beyond schooling* (pp.1029–1062). New York, NY: Rutledge.

He, M. F. & Phillion, J. (Eds.). (2008). *Personal~passionate~participatory inquiry into social justice in education.* Greenwich, CT: Information Age Publishing.

Mills, C. W. (1959). *The sociological imagination.* New York, NY: Oxford University Press.

Nussbaum, M. C. (2010). *Not for profit: Why democracy needs the humanities.* Princeton, NJ: Princeton University Press.

Perry, M. (2000). *Walking the color line: The art and practice of an urban high school.* New York, NY: Teachers College Press.

Robinson-Cole, C. (2007). *From the classroom to the corner: Female dropouts' reflections on their school years.* New York, NY: Peter Lang.

Schubert, W. H. (2009a). *Foreword.* In C. L. Carger, *Dreams deferred* (pp. xx–xxi). Charlotte, NC: Information Age Publishing.

Schubert, W. H. (2009b). *Love, justice, and education: John Dewey and the utopians.* Charlotte, NC: Information Age Publishing.

Schultz, B. D. (Ed.). (2010). *Listening to and learning from students: Possibilities for teaching, learning, and curriculum.* Charlotte, NC: Information Age Publishing.

Singham, M. (1998). The canary in the mine: The achievement gap between black and white students. *Phi Delta Kappan, 80*(1), 9–15.

Prologue

I teach a qualitative methods capstone course for social science majors at the community college where I work. Students choose their topics, frame their questions, design their methodological approach, and set out to do their work. It's not, of course, as linear as this. At the beginning of the semester I tell them that the projects that will produce the most powerful learning and bring them the most joy are those that begin with an unresolved story from their own lives. We talk about *continuity of experience* (Dewey, 1938): each of our experiences is fashioned by those that have come before, while at the same time altering the content and quality of those still to come. I encourage my students to explore something that has shaped them powerfully in the past, that continues to do so today, and that they wish to better understand and channel as they move forward.

My own life and the sense I make of it have been forged through my various experiences with public schooling. My most important identities—mother, "other mother," teacher, wife, and student—have been fleshed out on landscapes of schooling. When Ivan and Steve, two young people I've known for years, dropped out of high school, I *needed* to understand why. I was not intellectually curious, I was personally distraught. When I discovered that many young people in my community were making the same decision, my distress deepened and grew more urgent. My conversations with dropouts began in earnest, and they were imbued with resonance. My biography, as a child of the working class, as a mother raising children of privilege, and as a community college teacher, shapes the sense I make of these

Canaries Reflect on the Mine, pages xix–xxx

young people's stories. At the same time, their stories work both backwards and forwards on the sense I make of my own life.

* * *

The year was 1965, and my kindergarten teacher, Mrs. Keith, towered over the four and five-year olds in her charge. Perhaps she only seemed so tall because my mother was so short. Mrs. Keith loved a student named Helen. Helen had long, soft, curly brown hair, with red copper highlights. She always wore nice clothes—matching skirts, blouses, and knee socks, all crisp and clean. Her maturity and demeanor elevated her above everyone else. Helen was perfectly *contained,* and contained was a highly valued attribute in my kindergarten classroom. Mrs. Keith would regularly remark to the rest of us that we should behave more like Helen, and if she ever needed someone to run an errand, she *always* chose Helen. Perhaps you were such a child and can remember the exquisite joy of being the one your teacher trusted on a mission. I wasn't, and I didn't much like Helen, but mostly because Helen had no interest in liking me.

There was a second Helen in my class that year. She had very short, coarse black hair, with a cowlick in back and bangs that trailed north on one side. Her not-so-crisp-and-clean clothes were worn on a wiry thin body. This Helen was all elbows and legs in motion. She could disrupt the orderly quiet of the classroom in seconds, leaving children, art supplies, books and toys scattered in the winds. You did not want to get on the wrong side of one of those elbows. Mrs. Keith didn't like wiry Helen one little bit. Mrs. Keith didn't like me much either, but as bad as I felt most days, I knew that wiry Helen felt worse.

For reasons that made perfect sense to a five-year old, the difference between Mrs. Keith's treatment of the two Helens struck a distinctly discordant note with me. They shared a name after all; didn't that somehow make them equal? Because I had gotten on the wrong side of those elbows once or twice, I could appreciate Mrs. Keith's frustration, but her responses to Helen's various transgressions always seemed so much harsher than necessary. One day, after wiry Helen had gotten into more trouble than was usual, even for her, I asked my mother if she knew why Mrs. Keith loved one Helen but not the other. My mother remarked quite simply that Helen with the red copper highlights came from a "good" family and Helen with the cowlick did not. Now it's hard to describe exactly *how* my mother schooled me in the dynamics of social class and status, but like many mothers trending the wrong side of the divide, she started when I was very young.

Her own biography had produced a remarkably keen *sociological imagination* (Mills, 1959). Born in 1919, she was a Depression-era child from a working-class family who, although graduating second in her high school class, had neither the expectation nor the finances to go to college. She saved enough money to put herself through beauty school, and, except for a period during World War II when she labored in a munitions factory, she worked as a hairdresser her whole life. Good hairdressers are first and foremost excellent listeners. A stylist's abilities count, but customers become regulars as a consequence of their hairdresser's ears. My mother, a Christian with uncommonly progressive leanings for her time and place, deeply appreciated the wholeness, complexity, and fragility of people; she had a very good ear. My mother's "ladies" talked with her endlessly and fully about things big and small in their lives, and my mother listened closely. Much of my early socialization occurred sitting in a beauty shop listening to women talk. It was here that I learned a number of social graces. It's not polite, for instance, to ask an older person her age. It was here, also, that I learned more consequential cultural norms, such as not naming a teenager's unexpected death a suicide, and that young women *could* but never *should* have babies before they married.

Unlike wiry Helen's family, mine did not reside at the distant margins of the wrong side of the social class divide. We were poor, but we were not on welfare. We were not the norm, either. In our small town, where everyone knew everyone else, my mother divorced my father and set out to parent me alone. Although everyone knew of my otherwise gentle father's mean friendship with alcohol and weakness for women, divorce was just not something "good" people did in 1962 in my small town. Shortly after their divorce, my mother moved us to a two room space on Main Street. We slept in the back room; she did hair in the front. There was no kitchen, and when we weren't eating at my grandma's we ate at the diner next door. Al, one of the only black men in my rural hometown, regularly joined us at the counter.

My mother eventually remarried, moving us out of poverty and into a small house on the edge of town, but the stigmas of divorce and pink and blue collar labor continued to define our family in the eyes of "good" members of the community. When my mother schooled me on the difference between the two Helens, she was beginning to teach me how to navigate the wrong side of the social class divide. This lesson—repeated countless times in countless ways as I grew up—was a tangled paradox, a dance between the opposing realities of "right" and "good." From my mother's perspective, the different treatment of the two Helens was the opposite of right. In retrospect, I think that my mother was teaching me social class the way

Lisa Delpit (1995) suggests teaching "the language of power" to speakers of non-standard English. The aim is to teach competence with the standard form, while at the same time questioning its power. Similarly, my mother's challenge was to teach me how to play the game without becoming a player. There were rules I had to follow, even more closely than children from "good" families because my "bad" behavior would stand out more. If I felt compelled to break these rules, I needed to do so "under the radar." I *would* suffer injustices at the hands of teachers and administrators, but I should look at these as both instructive and character-building. Character building, because adversity would make me more resilient. Instructive, because how these injustices *felt in my shoes* should always shape how I treated other people. It was this second aspect of all her lessons that most strongly distinguished playing the game from becoming a player. Players forgot how injustice felt, and in the forgetting found it too easy to inflict it on others.

My experiences in kindergarten were repeated across my thirteen years in school (Anyon, 1980; Sennett & Cobb, 1973). Children like Helen and me had a few reprieves along the way, almost always with newly minted teachers who embodied the social justice leanings of their generation. It helped, also, if they had not been raised in our community. But there was one teacher, Mrs. Reed, who was neither young nor an outsider; she was just plain "right." Tall and pencil thin, with wispy brown hair, she always wore tailored suits, the jackets loosely fitted and the skirts straight as a ruler. On the face of it, she looked like she'd blow away in a strong wind, but she possessed a toughness, a grit, that belied her physical appearance. There were no elites in her English classes. Her expectations for our work, our interactions with her, and our behavior toward each other were extended to everyone alike. I cannot recall Mrs. Reed ever raising her voice, but she could deliver a withering look more powerful than any verbal correction. She devoted herself to our minds day in and day out, as we discussed Steinbeck, Hemingway, or Tolstoy. There were no lectures. She expected us to read the texts carefully and to share our impressions thoughtfully. She never substituted her understanding for ours, and she questioned us endlessly about how we had arrived at our interpretations. Sometimes I think I became a sociologist because I was raised in a beauty shop by my uncommon mother, and then schooled in *The Grapes of Wrath* by Lil Reed.

But Mrs. Reed was a member of a rare breed. In the eyes of most of my teachers, I was not going to amount to much. Like all perceptive adolescents, none of this was lost on me. By the time I was fourteen, although I was still following the spirit of my mother's charge to stay under the radar, I attended most classes stoned and did the minimum I needed to pass. During the mandatory "what should you do after high school?" conference with my guidance counselor my junior year, he suggested that my best bet was to "join the military." Except for English, my grades were unremarkable. He assured me the discipline would do me good.

For some reason, this particular indignity *really* pissed my mother off! To this day, I'm not sure why. Maybe she had just had enough. In any event, she made it clear that unless she had been living with a stranger for the last sixteen years, the military was no place for me. As this was the first and only time that my mother reacted to a school injustice, I took notice. I made an uneasy peace with the courses and teachers I disliked, restricted my pot-smoking to weekends, brought up my grades, and found myself heading to a four year state college at the end of my senior year.

College was amazing! The standardization movement had yet to creep into higher education, and my general education requirements consisted of an extremely flexible distribution across the arts and sciences. I had a ton of choices and was able to craft nearly all my coursework around my various interests. I graduated with a major in sociology, a minor in literature, and a passion for both history and philosophy. Because Mrs. Reed and my mother had taught me to read widely, to think deeply, and to write well, a number of professors—Don Wright, Robert Rhodes, John Marciano, and Frank Hearn—took a personal interest in my intellectual development and worked closely with me. I thrived. My mother was very proud, and in a most uncharacteristic on-the-radar move for her, she carried my grades around in her wallet on the chance that she would run in to my guidance counselor at the grocery store. She was apparently successful on several occasions. You'd have to have known my mother to appreciate how truly funny this image is; this was the same woman who remarked of her own status as salutatorian, "Well, we were a pretty dumb class on the whole."

While in graduate school, closely studying multiple forms of social inequality and processes of stratification, I fell in love with a man whose politics and larger world view resonated with my own. John was completing his teaching certification in elementary education, and when he started his Master's work, he chose Foundations of Education as his home. It's impossible to separate out my graduate studies from my partner's. When I discovered Paulo Freire, so did he. When he discovered John Dewey, Jean Jacques Rousseau, and Maxine Greene, so did I. What each of us was reading, thinking, and writing powerfully shaped the other.

John got his first teaching position in one of the poorest neighborhoods in a midsized city about 60 miles from where I was studying. We moved to a town slightly larger but very similar to the one I had grown up in. Located equidistant from his job and my graduate program, it offered us both a convenient commute, and, as a manufacturing town in decline, housing was cheap. When it came time to propose a dissertation topic, the decision to write an ethnography of John's urban elementary school seemed natural. Our first child and I were frequent visitors to his class. Not only did it offer a bounded milieu where I could explore class, race, and gender processes, it had recently adopted a reform model explicitly designed to challenge stratification: Continuous Progress. The idea behind Continuous Progress was to get rid of grades and retentions altogether, and to support each child's individual progress while keeping her with her age-mates.

Although this philosophy worked reasonably well within the walls of the school itself, it met crushing resistance beyond those walls. At the end of the reform's first year, the school's scores on the state mandated tests plummeted and it was placed on "The List." In the absence of grade retentions all eight year olds had taken the test. The results were disastrous. Three consecutive years on "The List" and a school would be taken over by the state or closed altogether.

Consequently, the year I was there, "grade of record" replaced the non-graded spirit of continuous progress, and the focus on the individual child was overshadowed by an insidious form of "social triage" (Books, 1994; Rubenstein, 1983; Sjoberg, Vaughan, & Williams, 1984). "Grade of record" was used to determine which children should be tested, and children considered most likely to score at a satisfactory level received the greatest share of instructional resources. Children not expected to score well were left largely to their own devices. Not surprisingly, test scores rose dramatically that year, and the school was removed from "The List" with much fanfare. A press conference and newspaper articles highlighted the remarkable success of Continuous Progress, all irony lost. My dissertation, which began as a hopeful study of the possibilities of authentic, individualized educational reform, morphed into a heartbreaking analysis of educational triage (Cameron, 1998, 2000; see also Michie, 2009) and "juking the stats," the bureaucratic practice of minimizing the appearance of misery depicted so brilliantly in the HBO series, *The Wire* (Simon, Colesberry, & Kostroff-Noble, 2002–2008).

That was twenty years ago, and No Child Left Behind and Race to the Top have only exacerbated the forces that dismantled Continuous Progress back then. Today, because my partner's urban school receives Reading First funding, he is forced to assess his second graders' literacy acquisition according to how many words they can accurately articulate in sixty seconds. And he must somehow get his students to perform this *trick* while he is simultaneously teaching them that reading is purposeful, that literacy is about pondering meaning and context—a process that asks one to slow down, not speed up (Keene & Zimmermann, 1997).

While writing my dissertation and teaching part-time at a local state college, a full-time sociology position opened at a nearby community college and I applied for it. When I was hired, I assumed it would be temporary. Like most Ph.D. candidates, I envisioned my "career" at a "real" college. But quite unexpectedly, my working class roots and I found a *home*. During my first year, my classes were populated with "underachieving" local high school graduates and GED earners as well as a significant number of adults who had recently been laid off from one of the last manufacturing plants in the area, a plant that left town to set up shop in Mexico. These students animated sociological concepts with such remarkable richness, stunningly rendering the dissonance between lives lived and cultural myths. They took my breath away. The icing on the cake was class size: 25 to 30 students instead of the 75 I was used to. After my first semester, I threw out my multiple choice tests and started to get to know my students. I have never once looked back.

Over these last 17 years, countless students have been my teachers (Freire, 1970; Ayers, 2001). From graduates of a nearby Coalition of Essential Schools high school, I have learned to shed my authority and welcome challenges to my knowledge. From an ever-growing number of home-schooled students, I have learned how powerful individualized care is to the development of voice. From non-traditional students, anxious and tentative about being "out of place," I have learned the value of tenacity. And from the many high school dropouts who have sat in my classes over these years, I've learned that the label never captures the complexity of the biography.

When I began teaching at the community college, my oldest child was just entering kindergarten, and my youngest was only ten months old. Developing as a teacher and as a parent have been tandem processes, each contributing to the other, and both contributing to my ever evolving understanding of schooling. For years I watched anxiously my children's different journeys from engaged learners to disenchanted students. My kids' early experiences with reading reflected the privileges of their birth. Their father is a gifted emergent literacy teacher, and we were able to provide them with a rich and varied home library and the gift of time made possible in a family supported by two living wage jobs. For years, reading together was the highlight of each day. Entering school, both children loved more than anything to be read to, and were primed to become readers themselves.

Nick was an early and voracious reader of picture books in kindergarten, but his real breakthrough, lending credibility to the Summerhill philosophy (Neill, 1992) of authentic need-driven learning, occurred in first grade. In literally a matter of days, he taught himself to read the popular *Goosebumps* books because an older child in his afterschool program had started a *Goosebumps* book club. Nick wanted more than anything to join it. Later that year, a teenager he idolized gave him her copy of Roald Dahl's *The Twits* (1980). He took it home, went directly to his room, and refused to go to sleep until he was done. When he finally allowed me to tuck him in for the night, he was transformed: "Mama, I'm never reading *Goosebumps* again!" Over the next several weeks, he read nearly every book Dahl had published for children.

Nick's turn away from reading, and ultimately school learning, began in third grade with his introduction to the Accelerated Reader (AR) program. Children read an AR-designated book, and then take a computerized multiple choice test that spits out their results, telling them whether they should read easier, similar, or more difficult books in the future. The emphasis of this program—like the Reading First assessments my partner is forced to use—is on quantity, not quality; superficial rather than deep learning. The "more" books a child reads, the more points she accumulates, the more perks and prizes she receives.

There are a multitude of problems with programs like Accelerated Reader, but the two that harmed Nick the most were the limitations it placed on his reading choices (only certain books have accompanying tests) and the convergent thinking it rewarded. When required to read a set number of books to "make the grade" but robbed of the power to choose widely, reading became a chore rather than a joy. Nick came home from school one day looking especially glum. When I asked what was wrong, he said, "I only got an eight out of 10 on *Abel's Island*" (Steig, 1976), and handed me the computer printout. Without looking at his test, I tried to reassure him: "8 out of 10? That's fine, sweetheart! Don't worry about it." With a note of resignation *so* uncharacteristic of this bright-eyed, exuberant boy, he responded, "But my teacher says I have to read easier books now." Nick had read *Abel's Island* independently for the first time two years earlier, and had been deeply moved by Abel's story of isolation. One of the questions he got "wrong" on his AR test was "How did Abel *feel* when he was alone on the Island?" The "correct" answer was "lonely." My child had chosen "sad."

Our daughter, Paige, followed her brother to the formal classroom environment five years later. Her turn away from schooling began in seventh grade, when she discovered that the creativity she had been allowed to exercise in her writing throughout elementary school was now unwelcome. About two months into the school year, Paige stormed through our front door and—in the first of what became frequent school-induced rages—hurled her books and notebooks across the entryway, screaming, "I can't write like this! I can't stand to read what I've written! It makes me sound like a moron!" If Accelerated Reader had robbed Nick of his love for reading, it was the TEES (topic, explain, example, summary) paragraph that transformed writing into a joyless exercise for Paige. Just as the complexity of Nick's interaction with Abel's isolation was reduced to one "incorrect" emotion on a multiple choice test, Paige's imaginative writing was wrestled into the straightjacket of a formula requiring her to produce a topic sentence, followed by an explanative sentence, followed by an example sentence, followed by a summary sentence. In a literacy autobiography she wrote in her first college writing course, she begins,

> I discovered at a young age that I loved English. I loved reading, being read to, writing stories, and just talking constantly. I credit this to my parents, who surrounded me with shelves and shelves of everything from Dr. Seuss to Arthur Miller, used an extensive language around me from the time I was born, and generally encouraged me to use my brain. Despite the fondness I developed so early for language arts, school was still able to strip me of the enjoyment I found.

Continuing on to describe the effects of TEES paragraph instruction, she writes,

> I was so limited in what I could write that I could stop using my brain altogether and wrote nearly identical sentences throughout the whole essay. For that year, writing was unbelievably easy, and unbelievably mundane.

Nick's alienation from school continued to grow each year, and my closest friends joke that getting him to the high school graduation platform was my second full-time job. I became his reluctant partner in a complicated dance designed to keep him out of trouble and in school enough days each year to accumulate the required number of Carnegie Units. Among other strategies, I threw regular fits when he refused to go to school, winning such confrontations about half the time; wrote countless fabricated and increasingly imaginative excuses for tardiness and missed days; conducted research on state graduation requirements and discovered that Comprehensive High (pseudonym) could not deny Nick a diploma because he had missed too many gym classes; and kept constant vigil over his graduation requirements and his progress each year. I had to have his schedule changed every year he was in high school so that he could graduate on time.

As my equally reluctant partner in the dance, Nick did just enough and not one bit more than was necessary to pass his required classes. His math grades were consistently poor, but he had mastered the skills he actually needed: basic percentages and how to calculate an average. When he was in danger of failing the required American History course due to absences and missed work, he got a 91 on the comprehensive final worth a fifth of the course grade, and scraped by with an average of 69. This was his modus operandi. Anything above the grade of C, in anything other than Concert Choir, was a sign of submission. Nick refused to submit.

At the same time Nick and I were engaged in this too often adversarial dance, I watched helplessly as some of his best friends, like Ivan and Steve whose stories appear later, made the life-altering decision to drop out of high school. These were young people I knew well. They had spent countless hours in my home over the years. Each one was bright, full of personality and promise. I was incensed!

When Paige entered ninth grade, one year after Nick had graduated and the same year I began talking with local dropouts, it was déjà vu on the home front. Before the first day of school, she was already negotiating the number of "mental health days" she would be allowed to take each month. By this time, I was becoming an arm chair expert on the sources of alienation at the local high school, and had wondered more than once whether the diploma Nick received had been worth, in Kirsten Olson's words, the "school wounds" he had endured (2009). Each conversation I had with a high school dropout that year only reinforced my sense that the costs of forcing Paige to remain at the high school were too high.

At the beginning of May in her freshman year, Paige stopped going to school altogether. She finished her coursework at home and then took the placement exams where I work, testing into freshman level math and English after only one year of high school. She began college as a high school dropout the following fall, at the age of fifteen.

Paige is smart and hard-working and I have an abiding respect for her bravery. Because traditional "school learning" was never difficult for her, it would have in some ways been easier to just stay in school, and she wrestles fiercely with the stigma of being a drop out. But Paige is also a child of privilege. The comparative ease of her transition from high school dropout to college honors student has as much to do with our family's resources as her natural abilities. Because she studies where I work, her tuition is free. But even if it weren't, we could afford to pay it. As important as this economic capital is, however, the cultural capital she has had at her disposal has been equally significant. The normative literacy skills she brought to the college placement tests were honed at home as well as at school. Imagining and then crafting a different route for her was made possible by John's and my critical understanding of compulsory schooling and our skills at navigating the daunting bureaucracy that serves it. Had Paige been born to a different family, like Hannah, whose story appears later, Comprehensive High might have filed a Person In Need of Supervision (PINS) petition against her. Her label, like Hannah's, might be juvenile delinquent instead of college sophomore. Many young people could benefit from the route Paige has taken, but few have the arsenal of resources required to do so.

Over the last few years, in addition to the many conversations I've had with local young people, I've read nearly every recent publication on U.S. dropouts. Sadly, it hasn't taken much of my time. The scope and complexity of the problem has not been met by a comparable research agenda. Most of what has been written has understandably focused on urban "dropout factories" where rates are highest (Tucci, 2009; see also Alliance for Excellent Education, 2009; Balfanz & Legters, 2004; Greene & Winters, 2002; Losen, 2004; Orfield, 2004; Richmond, 2009; Swanson, 2004), but I've found next to nothing on rural and small town contexts like mine (Hondo, Gardiner, & Sapien, 2008). And I've found even less research that systematically calls into question common stereotypes about dropouts (Bridgeland, DiIulio, Streeter, & Mason, 2008).

I suspect we would find defiance of these stereotypes around every corner if we spent more time talking to young people about their experiences and why they made the decision to leave school. In the U.S., the dearth of qualitative research from the perspective of dropouts themselves is simply remarkable when you think about it:

> When it comes to the topic of high school dropouts, there is a cacophony of voices participating in the conversation. There are teachers, administrators, school board members, and district superintendents. There are parents, politicians, school counselors and researchers. However, students are seldom involved in the conversation, especially students who either have dropped out of school or are thinking about it. (Knesting, 2008, p. 7; see also Christenson, Sinclari, Lehr, & Godber, 2001; Fredricks, Blumenfeld, & Paris, 2004; Gallagher, 2002; Lee & Breen, 2007)

This book adds the voices of a small group of dropouts to the larger cacophony. Three broad questions shaped the research: 1) How do these young people remember high school? 2) How did they arrive at the decision to drop out? 3) What changes would they make to the high school experience, if they had the power to do so? The answers to these questions are told through the stories of Iris, Hannah, Cole, Isabel, Adel, Ivan, and Steve (all pseudonyms). In writing these stories, I've tried to render the young people's experiences from their perspectives and, as much as possible, in their own words. I have done so not only out of respect for them, but because I believe that their insights are a precious gift to our understanding of schooling writ large. In the final analysis, their stories are not only about dropping out; they tell us also a good deal about the costs of persisting and the price of succeeding in our public school system.

According to the dominant narrative of schooling, the price of persistence, when considered at all, is thought of in only the most temporary and inconsequential of terms. Sure, school's no fun while you're in it, but if you're willing to "stick it out," to "delay gratification," you'll reap the rewards sometime in the future. This logic makes sense only when adolescence is viewed as a not fully human stage in the life cycle, a holding tank until real life begins. According to a perspective that denies the experiences and agency of living, meaning-making youth, we frame dropouts as reckless, misguided, lazy, or stupid. Recollecting the time shortly before his decision to walk out the school house door, Ivan captures this conventional wisdom powerfully: "I'm still *chugging* at it, though, 'cause high school's high school. What're you gonna do? You gonna drop out? Only fucking *losers* drop out of high school."

In stirring juxtapositions these young people defy the stereotypic frame, each one in completely different ways. And each one, like Ivan, struggles every day against the dominant identity we have crafted *for* them. This book is an invitation to join their struggle, an invitation to become more uneasy with comfortable truths about dropouts and less comfortable with the dominant narrative of schooling and success. We hope, in the end, that these stories will disrupt the reader's common sense as forcefully as wiry Helen's elbows and legs disrupted the contained quiet of Mrs. Keith's kindergarten classroom.

1

Narrative Research and Sociological Poetry

When we are young, the words are scattered all around us. As they are assembled by experience, so also are we, sentence by sentence, until the story takes shape.
—Louise Erdrich, 2008, p. 268

Sensibilities

This is a book of stories. Stories unfinished, stories still taking shape. Stories hopeful and heartbreaking at the same time. I've spent the last few years talking with young people about their lives, their school experiences, their decisions to drop out of high school, and their ideas for improving secondary education. My journey started with Ivan.[1] Ivan is my oldest child's friend. One day, as a junior in high school, my son came home and announced that Ivan had dropped out. I was stunned! Over the next couple of months, I had a series of conversations with friends who are teachers at the high school. I would ask, "What happened to Ivan?" And, in one way or another, they would tell me, "Ivan's just the tip of the iceberg. Kids are dropping like flies." Their responses drove me to the New York State Edu-

Canaries Reflect on the Mine, pages 1–16
Copyright © 2012 by Information Age Publishing
All rights of reproduction in any form reserved.

cation Department website and to the discovery that Comprehensive High School[2] really did have a "dropout problem."[3]

So I set out to do a bit of local action research. I believed that if I could better understand what was propelling students out of school in my community, I could—with their help—fashion some practical responses to share with the school board and district officials. But in the course of these overlapping and ongoing conversations, narratives that spoke to something more consequential than practical solutions began to take shape. These young people's stories were both unique and transcendent. They spoke of personal struggles, animating the lifeless statistics found in most U.S. research on dropouts. And they spoke to larger questions of power and purpose in the multi-layered, dissonant narrative of U.S. schooling. These were remarkable stories of ordinary lives.

How do I honor this gift? I wondered. These stories ached to be told, but my skills in academic discourse were proving woefully inadequate for expressing this ache. I was struggling mightily. And then I happened upon a letter C. Wright Mills had written to his friend, Dwight McDonald, in 1948 (in Summers, 2008), in which he described my struggle:

> Social scientists make up a rationale and a ritual for the alienation inherent in most human observation and intellectual work today. They have developed several stereotypical ways of writing which do away with the full experience by keeping them detached throughout their operation. It is as if they are deadly afraid to take the chance of modifying themselves in the process of their work. (pp. 33–34)

For Mills, this detachment is framed as the central problem, as *the* obstacle to understanding. His letter is a reaction to James Agee's and Walker Evan's *Let Us Now Praise Famous Men* (1939/2001), a study of southern sharecroppers during the Great Depression. Mills tells McDonald that the sharecroppers are brought to life by Evan's "magnificent" photographs and by Agee's prose, which, at its best, captures his "enormous furiosity" and his "crying terror" (Summers, 2008, p. 35). Reflecting on this work, Mills argued that social scientists should aim to craft *sociological poetry*, which he described as "a style of experience and expression that reports social facts and at the same time reveals their human meanings" (Summers, 2008, p. 34). In contrast to the "thick facts and thin meanings of the ordinary sociological monograph," sociological poetry, Mills said, rejects the dispassionate stance, adopting instead a "capacity for great indignation" (Summers, 2008, p. 35) and a willingness to be changed "in the process of [our] work"

(Summers, 2008, p. 34). Mills himself struggled to write sociological poetry his entire life (Mills, 2000). In the letter, he asks McDonald,

> How can a writer report fully the 'data' that social science enables him to turn up and at the same time include in his account the personal meanings that the subject often comes to have for him? Or: How can the writer master the detaching techniques necessary to modern understanding in such a way as to use them to feel again the materials and to express that feeling to the readers? (Summers, 2008, p. 33)

"Okay," I said to myself, "Mills struggled with this problem. This problem itself is transcendent." I felt better. I kept writing. And the academic voice spoke more quietly and less often. A few months after discovering Mills' letter, I went to the annual meetings of the American Educational Studies Association and had an opportunity to attend a book chat given by William Ayers. My Foundations of Education students and I read something that Ayers has written every semester. I love his work. I was a captive audience. In the conversational style so engaging in his books, he encouraged his audience to "write into the contradiction" and to reject the binary separations of head and heart, mind and body. The time to research and write with passion is always *now*, he asserted. I came home; the academic voice now reduced to an occasional whisper, I began to lovingly write something that I hope approaches honoring the ache and the desire these young people shared with me.

The Town and the School

The stories take place in a small city, more rural than urban, in upstate New York. The town has a population of roughly 18,000. Ninety-five percent of residents are white (U.S. Census Bureau, 2005–2009).[4] Once a robust manufacturing town, home to both factory owners in breathtaking Victorian mansions on tree lined avenues and factory workers in humble single family homes in quiet residential neighborhoods, the town has over the last century witnessed the decline in locally owned businesses, the rise in national and multinational industries, and finally—over the last thirty years— the devastating effects of deindustrialization (Bluestone & Harrison 1984; Weis, 1990, 2004; Wilson, 1996). One living-wage industry after another has either gone bankrupt or left this small city for cheaper labor elsewhere. The town is home to a public college, with jobs in education, health care, and social services making up 33.5% of all employment (U.S. Census Bureau, 2005–2009). In an increasingly common narrative, a recent fight over the construction of a Super Walmart pitted underemployed working-class residents against local college professors and environmentalists. Walmart won.

Henry, one of the young people who talked with me, situates the dropout problem within this larger economic context:

> I mean, this is a pretty dead town, a lot of like lower income families. We have a lot less money than the towns around us do. We have a lot of like, I can't even think of the right word to use here, but do you kinda get what I'm trying to say here? Like a lot of the poorer families, and then we have the projects up on the hill there. I think it just might be that we have more situations like that [than other towns]. That might just be the issue, and not the school itself. I really don't think it's a problem with Comprehensive High as much as it's just high schools in general, and then kinda like exacerbated by the town being a pretty dead town.

In 2009 inflation-adjusted dollars, median household income was just below \$38,000, and the mean just above \$48,000. Thirty-six percent of households had an annual income of less than \$25,000. Eleven percent of all families were living below the poverty line. Eighteen percent of families with children under the age of 18 fell below the poverty line, and 21% of families with children under the age of five did so. In female headed households, poverty rates for families with children under the ages of 18 and five were 37% and 49%, respectively (U.S. Census Bureau, 2005–2009).

The town is served by one comprehensive high school. Between 2007 and 2010, Comprehensive Junior Senior High served roughly 1,300 students each year in grades seven through twelve, with an average class size of 20 in core subjects in eighth and tenth grades. The racial composition of students during the same time period was approximately 90% white, 6% African American, and 3% Latino. Students with limited English proficiency did not exceed 1% during any of these years (New York State Education Department, 2009–2010a). Average per pupil expenditure in the district between the years 2005 and 2008 was close to \$13,000, compared to the state average of just above \$16,000 (New York State Education Department, 2005–06, 2006–07, 2007–08).

There is a very small, public alternative high school that offers an intimate and supportive environment for the small number of students who attend, although its funding was recently reduced significantly as a consequence of the state's broader economic challenges. Other than a small religious school, there are no private high schools in the city. Although a small number of students attend private schools in a nearby metropolitan area, most of the town's young people attend Comprehensive High School.

One consequence of this is significant social class heterogeneity within the student population. Between 2007 and 2010, 21% of students were eligible for free lunch and another 7% were eligible for reduced lunch (New York State Education Department, 2009–2010a). During those same years, the percent of children in families receiving public assistance was estimated to be between 21 and 30 (New York State Education Department, 2007–08, 2008–09, 2009–2010b).

Social class figured prominently in the stories of nearly all of the young people in this study, and most spoke about an entrenched stratification system at Comprehensive High reminiscent of William Chambliss's classic study *The Saints and the Roughnecks* (1973). References to the "preps" and the "jocks" were made repeatedly, and most of the young people believed that students with money, athletic talent, or the ability to perform well academically were valued more highly and given greater resources—including the benefit of the doubt—than others. This is, of course, not a new story.

The Young People and the Process

Twelve young people shared their experiences with me: five women and seven men. Eleven are white and one is African American. Two of the twelve come from solidly middle class households and the remaining from families experiencing a range of economic difficulties. The economic challenges are related to the poor labor market prospects of parents and guardians within the context of deindustrialization and to the disruption of household income-pooling caused by divorce and separation. Only three of the young people come from families that are "intact" in the traditional sense. Their ages at the time of their initial interviews ranged from 15 to 21. The bulk of the data was gathered in semi-structured interviews. Individuals were paid twenty dollars for each interview. Additional data came from countless informal conversations, emails, Facebook exchanges, and text messages. Our conversations began in early 2009, and in the case of six participants, continue to this day.

The young people came to me in a variety of ways, and this study has benefited enormously by a web of social relationships that was instrumental in encouraging them to share their stories frankly. Most of the participants were referred to me by the assistant director of a local community youth organization, Susan, who runs a GED program. Susan has worked for this organization for thirty years. During that time, approximately 3,000 young people have come through her door seeking GED preparation, and more than 1,000 have gone on to earn their equivalency degrees. Her advocacy for community youth is legendary in this town. Most important for this study, she is trusted by the young people with whom she works. She created a bridge between them and me. A bridge built of love and dedication. A bridge that felt firm and safe to cross.

Although I had known of Susan's work for years, I had never actually met her. A former student of mine, Laura, shares a close personal relationship with both Susan and me. Laura is herself a high school dropout, and Susan's mentorship and support were essential to her completion of a GED. Years later, Laura ended up in one of my introductory sociology sections, the first of several classes she took with me. She went on to complete her AS in social sciences and her BA in sociology. Through the years we've remained close. When I told her I wanted to talk with local high school dropouts, she introduced me to Susan.

Susan and I discovered in each other the same social justice leanings animating our thinking and agency with respect to youth. She was very excited about the study and began immediately emailing and snail-mailing me information that she had been collecting for years. She reviewed and made important contributions to my interview questions. When I was ready to begin interviewing, she provided priceless support. Not only did she give me a list of names and contact information for recent Comprehensive High dropouts who had applied to her GED program, she sent each one of them a personal letter introducing me as her friend and encouraging them to participate in the study. Her advocacy gave me a level of credibility at the outset that I would never have had otherwise.

Eight of the twelve young people were recruited by Susan, but in four of those cases, encouragement to participate came from others they trusted as well. The first two people I interviewed were David and Hannah. Both had older siblings who had dropped out before them, and both of these siblings had received letters from Susan as well. David and Hannah liked being interviewed and encouraged their siblings to contact me. Within days of these interviews, I received calls from David's sister, Isabel, and Hannah's brother, Henry.

In another case, my phone messages to a potential participant had gone unanswered for months. One day, seemingly out of nowhere, Nathan called me and said he wanted to be interviewed. This struck me as a little odd. Why now? But when he showed up, he was with Cole, whom I had recently interviewed. Cole told him to go ahead and do it, drove him to the interview, and waited in another room while we talked. Nathan enthusiastically told his story, and I can only attribute his demeanor and frankness to Cole's encouragement.

Another participant is the sister of one of my students. After discussing my research in class one evening, this student asked me if I would interview Iris, who, it turns out, had also received Susan's letter. With her sister's encouragement, Iris agreed to participate; again, the richness of the initial interview suggested that she was operating on a level of basic trust.

Jamie was referred to me by the daughter of one of my best friends. Within a week of his leaving school, she texted him my phone number and told him to contact me. About a week after that, I received a phone call from Cole, who said, "Hey, I've got another one for you." It turned out to be Jamie, who now had two friends encouraging him to participate.

The final three participants—Steve, Ivan, and Emily—I have known for years, through my children's circles of friends.

I viewed these conversations as gifts from the very start, taking my time with each one. Because I was on sabbatical, I had the luxury of conducting no more than one interview a week, and of spending the next several days transcribing and reflecting on each conversation. Once I had completed a transcription I sent it to the participant, along with a personal thank you letter, and, in a number of cases, information requested about programs at the college where I teach.

My initial plan had been to analyze the interviews using constant comparison (Glaser & Strauss, 1967), looking backward and forward in order to identify common themes and experiences (Lincoln & Guba, 1985; Mayan, 2009). After I had completed the first five interviews, I created matrices of responses around topic areas and began coding the discourse and looking for patterns. A number stood out easily. However, the dominant theme to emerge from every conversation was each young person's sense that their school experiences and relationships neglected the complexity of their lives and minimized them as individuals. They felt they were not *known* as whole persons, and not being known was an overarching factor in their decisions to leave school early.

In his beautifully crafted memoir, *Holler if You Hear Me* (2009), Greg Michie describes a project he worked on with five Latina middle-school students in Chicago. With his assistance, the five produced an audio book of dramatic readings of Sandra Cisneros' vignettes from *The House on Mango Street* (1991). The narrator of the vignettes is Esperanza. Of working and learning with the girls, Michie (2009) writes, "As the days and weeks passed, I got to know more about each of the girls' singular stories and sensibilities. Each of them may have been Esperanza, but each was Esperanza in her own unique way" (p. 64). This is how I felt as I considered the young people and their stories. Yes, each was a dropout, but each was a dropout in her or his own unique way.

The more I focused on the matrices I was constructing, the more uneasy I felt. Yes, there were clear patterns. Yes, there were sufficient data across multiple transcripts to document those patterns. But the matrices neglected the unique biographies, experiences, and insights that each person offered. Too much was getting lost in translation as I metaphorically cut these young people up, dissecting them piece by piece. The entire process *felt wrong*.

So I took a break from the matrices and began writing each participant's story separately. At first, my only purpose for doing so was to create a separate space in my own mind for each young person. When I thought about Hannah in relation to Jamie, or Steve in relation to Ivan, I wanted to see their common experiences without losing the richness of their individual biographies, and how this richness shaped the quality and perception of those experiences. Around this time, I discovered Mills' letter to McDonald and began a novice's attempt at transforming chronological events into sociological poems. Shortly after, I attended Ayers' book chat. From that moment on, I gave myself permission to enter into the process, to shake off the detached stance, and to really believe in the larger value of the individual stories.

Two forces coalesced as I re-engaged with the materials this way. First, and paradoxically, as my gaze moved away from discrete comparisons to seeing each young person whole, the existential connections of each one's story to the others became clearer. Although I did not yet have a name for the method I was employing, in retrospect I see that I was discovering in an emergent and authentic way that "One person's story, analyzed in sufficient depth, represents a larger collection of social experiences" (Mayan, 2009, p. 49; see also Goodall, 2008). I had discovered the power of the narrative. Second, I found myself writing joyfully. Once the process ceased feeling like an academic exercise to report "findings," and became, instead, an artful and loving rendering of lives, I was drawn to rather than repelled by the keyboard. Hours of uninterrupted writing passed effortlessly.

Seven of the twelve stories appear in this book. They were selected not only for the unique insights they add to the conversation on dropping out, but also because I'm fairly confident that they capture the experiences and points of view of the people for whom they speak. Isabel's story is the only one that is based on a single conversation. Between our interview and my attempts to reconnect with her, she moved and her phone was disconnected. I have not been able to locate her again. My misgivings about sharing her story without the benefit of her feedback are tempered by the quality of her interview, in which she shared in a remarkably frank and brave way the experience of social class and academic marginalization. Cole's story is based on a single interview and several informal conversations. The remaining five stories—Hannah's, Adel's, Iris's, Ivan's, and Steve's—reflect the varying degrees of ownership asserted by each of them. In all five, the stories have been read by their protagonists, and each has provided feedback, made corrections, added information, and affirmed the truth of the final telling.

Ivan's and Steve's stories are particularly rich with respect to detail and narrative, due to the longevity of our relationships and my regular interactions with them. Both are friends of my son and both served as personal catalysts for this work. From the moment of our first conversation about dropping out to our frequent exchanges today, Ivan's fierce desire to analyze his experiences has shaped his participation. He desperately wanted to make sense of how an "honors kid"—a kid who knew how to *do school* and was able to do school with ease—could end up a dropout. He has revised his own story multiple times, read others' stories, provided priceless feedback on the analytical chapters, and sat quietly in the audience at conferences where I've presented work from this study. I'm still trying to coax him to present with me.

Steve's and my relationship has been the most personally transformative for us both. Although he had been a frequent presence in my home, even living for a while on the third floor, for years our friendly interactions never broke the surface. Flash forward a year after our first interview, and I receive the following text: "Happy mothers day . . . I hope you have a wonderful day. Thanks for being there when I needed someone to talk to. I'm thankful for the people I have in my life." Our first interview sparked a connection that has evolved over time into a deeply and reciprocally valued "other mother–son" relationship. A word that Steve loves, and that he might use to describe what transpired during that conversation and what it led to, is serendipity.

Facebook, email, and text-messaging have been indispensable tools in the process. Since our first interviews, Hannah, Ivan, and Iris have moved around a lot. But they all check their Facebook accounts regularly. Each time I revised one of their stories, I would text them or send a Facebook message to let them know I'd emailed a new draft. Usually within a day or two, I'd have their feedback.

All five of these young people agreed in broad strokes with even those first drafts and were generally happy with them. In retrospect, I believe that two qualities helped me to get the gist of their stories mostly right on

the first try. The first is my own sensibility toward youth, which is simultaneously grounded in the historical and critical tradition of the sociology
of C. Wright Mills (1959; see also Horowitz, 1963; Mills, 2000; Summers,
2008) and my vivid memories of my own adolescence. When I hear the
phrase "kids these days," it doesn't conjure the typical response. I *like* young
people. I enjoy their company and I have an abiding respect for their perspectives. I have no expectation for them to act like I did at their age, because they have come of age within a very different historical context. Consequently, when they tell me something that sparks dissonance, it sparks my
curiosity just as strongly. I believe the initial stories I wrote reflected this
sensibility. They were deeply respectful, and the young people recognized
that. Each one could find at least one place in his or her story where he or
she felt I had captured something both perfectly and poetically. Referring
to one such passage, Hannah said, "I was like, *oh man*, you know, that's *really*
how I'm saying it, I thought that was probably one of the strongest points
in the story. [Pause]. And I just think the whole thing is definitely how I
woulda told it." Referring to a passage in his story, Ivan said, "There's this
part in the middle where when I'm talking about my favorite teachers and
you couldn't really see why [I liked them so much], and then you realized
it, and then the way you um, the way you worded it was, I put, 'perfect'."
Feeling affirmed, they developed more trust and this served as an invitation
to continue our work together.

The second quality that I brought to the writing of their stories is a
wide and deep knowledge of the history and contradictory impulses of
public schooling in the U.S. Conflict-ridden and context-rich, my knowledge supported each young person's desire to expand her or his self-con-
scious identity. Every day, these young people live the stigma that is at-
tached to the label "dropout." Each one, in her or his own way, struggles
fiercely in the ever-shifting space between the one-dimensional identity
our society has crafted for dropouts—"fucking loser" (Ivan), "worthless
failure" (Steve), "stupid" (Iris), "lazy" (Hannah)—and a quiet yet persistent voice that knows this identity is shallow and false, unjust and unde-
served. Nearly all of the interviews spoke to the experience of carrying the
burden, thick and heavy, of the socially constructed identity. At the same
time, every interview spoke to a multi-dimensional lived experience that
defies this identity. The juxtaposition between the dominant narrative of
school leaving and their experiences of leaving school is irreconcilable.
Living the tension is deeply painful. My critical understanding of schooling supported each one's desire to affirm the tenuous counter-identity
that whispered beneath the spin in each one's consciousness. Together, we

complicated and contracted the dominant identity and enlarged the space for the counter-identity to root and grow.

This process continued from one draft to the next. After several iterations, Ivan, finally satisfied with the final product, sent me an email. He wrote "Hit it dead on" in the subject heading, and said, "I feel like *I* didn't even understand my own standpoint until I read this." Steve's final feedback, in a Facebook exchange, captures the collaborative identity construction and expanding understanding of self and context that we co-authored.

> I'm pretty sure that you're one of the few people that more or less totally understand me. You really know how to dig deep and understand people. I think you did a great job at representing me and it's a tough task (maybe impossible) to try to represent anyone in general, but for the schooling aspect you totally transformed my emotions to paper. What happened with my mom is just one story . . . and everyone has a story, but the truth is few will be told. I'm glad that you helped me with this obstacle that's been haunting me throughout my life, and through you I have faced my own reality and have now looked beyond it. People tend to be afraid of their pasts, and quite honestly I don't blame them, but there comes a time and place to face yourself, and to face who you truly are. Until then, it will always be a mystery, an unsolved puzzle. More like a jigsaw puzzle with missing pieces that is impossible to completely solve even at your fullest potential. I'm not afraid anymore, and for that I thank you. Once you understand the game, and what the levels and rules of the game are, then the world isn't a trick anymore. (personal communication, May 26, 2011)

The young people's appreciation for the *substance* of the first drafts of their stories contrasted sharply with their significant concern about the mechanics of how they sounded. I had not edited the transcripts; their words and mine appeared on the page exactly as spoken. My first follow-up interview was with Hannah. After she told me how much she liked her story, I asked whether she would change anything. She responded, "On some of 'em I saw, like, it's written 'woulda'—was I really saying 'woulda' or was I saying 'would of,' 'cause I don't normally say woulda." In what would be the first of many such responses, I said that everyone speaks in nonstandard form and pointed this out in my own spoken word. Hannah responded, "Okay, okay, well in my head I'm saying 'would of,' but maybe it comes out as 'woulda.'" It was important to her that I recognize that and she was concerned about her credibility with a larger audience.

Following Hannah, each person shared concerns about how they sounded. Steve, for instance, said, "Funny thing is, I never even noticed how much, what I say over and over—'You know what I mean'—I said it, how many times did I say it? I never, I never even realized it until I read it. I said it so many times." Henry's concern was over his use of the term "like." Similarly, Iris's responded to what became the near-final version of her story: "I think I say 'like' too much and it would be awesome if you could fix that. Otherwise I like it."

While conducting the follow-up interviews, I would share with each person what the others were saying. We would talk about experiences they shared, how they responded to those experiences, and their overall reactions to the stories I had written. By the time I had completed all of the follow up interviews, I could no longer minimize the concern about nonstandard language. Ivan's observation captures eloquently the collective response to this issue. In an email, he writes,

> As for the debate over whether or not to clean up some of the dialog, I can see why most of us would be for it. A word-for-word transcription of a face-to-face interview is bound to have some 'on the spot' answers that are not completely thought out or put in correct grammatical form. Now that we've had some time to review the things we said, it is no surprise that we would want to tweak our answers this way or that, or just clean them up a little. The big question is whether or not cleaning up these responses compromises the factuality or credibility of these interviews. I don't think it does. If I, or we, are at this point able to put forth a better way to more clearly express our points of views, or if some unnecessary "you knows" or "likes" are omitted, I don't think they will be missed or questioned. (personal communication, March 14, 2011)

This universally shared and doggedly persistent objection became a catalyst not only for how I handled their concerns, but for deeper reflection about voice in the telling of marginalized lives. In terms of qualitative research more generally, it raises important questions about representation and ownership. Who has the final say about language in the telling of the stories? Out of respect for their concerns, I cleaned up the transcripts, never adding to their words, but editing out many of the "ahs," "ums," "likes," and in Steve's case, I've significantly reduced the number of times he says, "You know what I mean?" Each person welcomed these changes.

In addition to issues of representation, their reactions raise fundamental questions about the validity of the standardized assessments we use to measure students' skills with standard communication forms. Assessments that are decontextualized and absent student purpose may significantly under-measure student skills and students' ability to code-switch. Most of the young people in this study come from working class backgrounds with no family history of higher education. They speak in nonstandard forms, like most of us. They also do school and school-based assessments using nonstandard forms of communication. Yet they demonstrate considerable recognition of standard forms in the reading and editing of their stories and transcripts. I suspect that at least two factors account for this. First, they know their stories. They're not being asked to talk about something for which they have neither expertise nor interest. Second, they care deeply that the audience understand and appreciate what they're saying. Although each one had a desire to present him or herself in a good (read "smart") light, and therefore did not want to come across as sounding uneducated or "dumb," their investment extended beyond their individual representations. From the first interview to the last conversation, each one hoped that their story might improve schooling for others. They saw this work as important, and they understood that how they sounded would support or challenge their credibility with some audiences.

As a consequence of what I've learned in this process, my introductory sociology students now spend the entire semester writing, revising, and finally performing autoethnographic narratives (Cameron, forthcoming). I encourage them to expand and deepen their voices, and to use nonstandard forms when these best express their experiences. They often mindfully braid the standard and nonstandard together, and what has been consistent is the agility and clarity of their language and voice. They have hands down produced the best writing I've encountered among undergraduate students. Like the young people in this study, my students are experts on their experiences, and they have a vested interest in performing successfully for their audience. They experience "purpose" in the Deweyan sense of the word (1938): The endeavor is important to the doer, calls for reflection on past observations to make sense of the present, and offers the opportunity to shape the future. It is an activity of *significance*, consciously recognized as such by the person undertaking it. In Dewey's (1938) words, "a purpose is an end-view" (p. 6).

Traditional critiques of qualitative research will be raised by this work. How good is the memory? How honest the tale? How representative the experience? In taking this work on the road to conferences, I'm often asked about "the other side" of the story; how would the teachers and administrators at Comprehensive High tell the tale? I suspect they would tell it quite differently, but I don't think that detracts from the value of these stories. The gap between teachers' intentions and students' perceptions is often vast, and the too rarely explored stories of students help us to better understand why that is. In this research, when asked what they most liked about school, each participant responded with stories about teachers who cared well for them. Significantly, specific teachers were also identified by each one in response to what they least liked about school. Moreover, the same

teacher was sometimes named as the best thing about school by one participant and the worst by another. The teacher Ivan identifies as one catalyst in
his decision to drop out is also credited by another young person I know as
the key reason she persisted to graduation. Overall, the experiences these
young people had with their various teachers support Noddings' (2005)
argument that the teacher-student relationship, whenever possible, should
be consensual.

Another likely critique of this work—the unresolved and contingent
nature of the stories and their meanings—speaks also to its promise. No
matter how well my partners and I have worked to collaboratively write
these tales, no matter how seriously we've taken the charge to craft sociological poems, these stories only begin to capture the multidimensionality
and full human meaning of the lives they represent. James Agee (Agee &
Evans, 2001) captures this idea beautifully in the preamble to *Now Let Us
Praise Famous Men*:

> In a novel, a house or a person has his meaning, his existence, entirely
> through the writer. Here, a house or a person has only the most limited of
> his meaning through me: his true meaning is much huger. It is that he *exists*,
> in actual being, as you do and as I do, and as no character of the imagina-
> tion can possibly exist. His great weight, mystery, and dignity, are in this fact.
> As for me, I can tell you of him only what I saw, only so accurately as in my
> terms I know how; and this in turn has its chief stature not in any ability of
> mine but in the fact that I too exist, not as a work of fiction, but as a human
> being. Because of his immeasurable weight in actual existence, and because
> of mine, every word I tell of him has inevitably a kind of immediacy, a kind
> of meaning, not at all necessarily 'superior' to that of imagination, but of a
> kind so different that a work of imagination (however intensely it may draw
> on 'life') can at best only faintly imitate the least of it. (pp. 9–10, emphasis
> in original)

Although some may see this as a weakness, I see it as profoundly hopeful.

Organization of the Book

The heart of this book consists of the seven individual stories spoken about
previously. Chapter 2 is Hannah's story, capturing a juxtaposition of vulnerability and tenacity in almost equal measure. Whispering painfully, "I wasn't
golden," she speaks to the stratification and unequal valuing of peer groups
in school. Alongside this wound of exclusion, Hannah asserts a stubborn
claim to just treatment and a mindful agency in its absence: "You're not
gonna respect me, you're not getting *any* respect from me!"

In Chapter 3, borrowing Forrest Gump's metaphor for life, Steve says that school is "a box of chocolates. You never know what you're gonna get. Sometimes school can mess with you, sometimes it helps you out." He invites the reader to look at the world through the eyes of a professional gambler, not an addict played by the game, but a disciplined and fearless player who displays an uncommon ease with random forces and a hard-won confidence in his ability to remain standing after suffering devastating hands.

In Chapter 4, Adel speaks to the relationship between retention and dropping out, disrupting the conventional frames of "passing students along" verses "holding students accountable," in which teachers are responsible to the curriculum rather than to the students themselves. Adel reframes retention as pedagogy that is both respectful and alert to students, promoting the development of community and deep learning for all classroom participants.

Chapter 5 is Cole's tale. Coming from a tumultuous home life and virtually independent since the age of thirteen, Cole's is a story of dissonance: being treated like a child in school while he's "out on [his] own" everywhere else. Simultaneously infantilizing him and offering nothing of tangible value to help him meet his real needs as a young person with little support, school is an obstacle to Cole's survival.

Of school, Isabel observes, "It was pretty much like I felt I wasn't even there." In Chapters 6 and 7, Isabel and Iris tell stories of invisibility and silencing. Each believes in the value of an education, each wants desperately to be educated, and each one is thwarted in her pursuit. Their stories illustrate how a narrowly constructed, normative definition of "student," and of what it means to "do school," denies many young people a rightful place in their classrooms, undermining their success and making them painfully vulnerable in relationships with both peers and teachers. Their stories also suggest that the costs of neglect and invisibility extend beyond those who are not seen and heard to those who "do school" with ease.

In Chapter 8, Ivan tells his story. A member of the gifted program, enrolled in honors and Advanced Placement classes, and fully engaged in a wide range of extracurricular activities, Ivan was, for years, a "model" student. And then he wasn't. He talks about the "point in time where [he] just stopped believing in high school," identifying clearly the factors that resulted in his "loss of faith." His story disturbs the dominant narrative of schooling by revealing some of the unspoken costs of success.

Chapter 9 is the product of constant comparison and identifies the transcendent themes that emerged from the study: the desire to be *known* and *valued* and the need to act with *purpose* and *autonomy*. Challenging conventional wisdom about dropouts as *losers*, these themes frame dropouts as *canaries in a coal mine*. For a multitude of reasons, dropouts are especially sensitive to the various toxins that pervade schooling. As such, they offer remarkable insights about the existential costs of schooling to the wellbeing of *all* students.

Chapter 10 juxtaposes the dominant discourse on schooling (the spin) with a progressive social justice and democratically oriented alternative (the whisper), one that speaks to the meaning these young people have made. Spin and whisper evoke the same "cherished values" (Mills, 1959, p. 11) equity and justice, but they are framed quite differently by each. Within the spin, equity and justice are reduced to offering children and youth standardized, externally derived educational inputs and assessments, animated by an impoverished capitalist and bureaucratic "efficiency." The whisper, in contrast, frames justice and equity as educational practices that lovingly embrace and extend students' experiences, enrich their biographies, and celebrate and support each of their talents and purposes with equal passion.

2

Hannah

Pushing Back, Moving On

T he first time I meet Hannah, it's a cold, but not too cold, January day, and she's wearing a trendy fitted jacket and knit cap. With sparkling hazel eyes and pierced lips and nose, she is *lovely*. At nineteen, she's spunky, insightful, and eloquent. She speaks with both expression and confidence, as she projects a strong sense of self, sharing with me the underlying significance of her first name and promptly correcting my mispronunciation of her last name. To my delight, Hannah is not the least bit deferential toward me. She owns and animates her power, co-constructing a conversation between equals. Throughout the first interview, two characteristics stand out: a fierce determination to exert control over her own life, and a quiet sadness about those contexts in which such control eludes her. She paints a portrait of tenacity and vulnerability.

Writing her story the first time is easy; although there are gaps in what I know about her experiences, I feel as if I have a sense of her. When we sit at my kitchen table four months later to talk about the story I've written, she tells me, "I just think the whole thing is definitely how I would tell it." When

Canaries Reflect on the Mine, pages 17–24

asked if she would change anything, she takes exception to my rendering of her vernacular, which assaults her recognition of standard conventions. She wants the reader to know, for instance, that she recognizes that "woulda" is not a standard construction. Hannah's sense of self is even more striking during this second conversation, as she fills in what's missing.

The daughter of two health care professionals who divorced when she was four, Hannah lived with her dad for most of her childhood and attended a neighborhood elementary school in the Comprehensive School District, where she was a strong student. Because there is nothing in her first interview to suggest *any* academic struggles like those chronicled by Isabel, Iris, or Adel, I ask specifically about this during our second conversation.

> **Jeanne:** The sense that I got was that the kind of help you wanted from teachers was less academic [Yeah] and more emotional [Yeah!]. So—academically—did you feel like you could pretty much take care of business?

Hannah responds with confidence, and also as a matter of fact, "*Yeah, I'm smart!* And I know I'm smart. I mean I didn't do my *homework*, but I didn't need that kind of help."

If young people could leave their out-of-school lives outside the school house door and if school culture didn't punish kids whose lives complicate their school experiences, Hannah would have graduated. The kind of help Hannah most needed, like Steve and Cole, was someone to *see* her needs, to listen—*really listen*—to what was going on in her life and to support her. At fourteen, like many adolescents, Hannah started to get into trouble:

> It kinda had to do with school, but it also kinda didn't. There was a lot of other things going on, but when I was fourteen, I was skipping school 'cause I didn't wanna be there, so I got put on probation—PINS [Person in Need of Supervision] first—and then I kept skipping.

Hannah's troubles outside of school coincided with her entry into ninth grade or high school. The elementary schools in the district are small neighborhood schools and families are encouraged to be involved. The junior high, which is housed in the same building as the high school, is self-contained and structured according to a team approach. Young people are divided—heterogeneously—among four teams: two teams for seventh grade and two for eighth. Team teachers plan curriculum together, and, as importantly, collaboratively support student progress. Like several other young people in this study, Hannah loved her junior high team teachers.

Once a young person enters ninth grade, however, collaboration among teachers and unified support for kids breaks down. So, at precisely the time that Hannah's out-of-school problems began, her in-school support structure broke down. She responded by skipping school. Comprehensive School District responded in turn by filing the PINS petition over her pervasive absenteeism—"I skipped about the last three months of school. And I didn't take my, uh, finals [Laughs]." This landed Hannah back in ninth grade for another year, only this time she was a ninth grader who had "failed" and who now had a reputation as a "bad kid." She continued to skip school regularly, and, as a result, was put on probation. After this, she says, "I did well for awhile, and then I just started skipping school again."

Outside of school, lots of stuff was happening. Her father fell in love with a woman, and they moved their respective families together. And, following a common narrative, the blended family was fraught with conflict. Hannah refused to make nice; Hannah's father asked her to leave. Like multiple slices of Hannah's narrative, she straddles a sense of righteousness on the one hand and rejection on the other.

> He only kicked me out because, you know, he had a new girlfriend and I *hated* her son and I couldn't deal with it anymore, so [dad] was just like, "Just go, just go." So, I mean it really didn't bother me at all. I was like, hey, I get to go live with my mom. Like it was a better time.

Living with her mom was "a better time," but only for awhile. Hannah continued to opt out of a hostile school culture that had labeled her "bad," refused often to follow her mother's rules, and became involved in "a bad relationship." It was this relationship to which Hannah attributes her eventual placement in foster care—"I got with this guy who was *not good*, and then he caused me to go into foster care." Her mother, feeling that Hannah was out of control, filed a PINS petition herself. This resulted in Hannah's removal from the home. Again, Hannah's rendering acknowledges her mother's sense of helplessness and Hannah's own lack of cooperation, on the one hand, and expresses an underlying sense of abandonment on the other.

> I was removed at sixteen. My mom also filed a PINS on me after the school did. Because I wasn't listening to them either. So my mom—my dad had kicked me out at fifteen, so he *really* didn't care—but my mom, it hurt her to see me go, but, it wasn't, it wasn't mainly school related why I went, but so she was like "It's *best* for you ... to go" [mild sarcasm].

Although her foster care placement wasn't mainly school related, Hannah's subsequent experiences attending two other schools while in foster care tell a story of how schooling can support or challenge further a young person in trouble. Hannah was first assigned to a very small rural school, a school she remembers with love. It was composed of kindergarten through twelfth grade, and there were often no more than twelve or thirteen students in a class. The average graduating class was about 40 students. The small size of both town and school promoted a sense of belonging and community. When asked what she liked about this school, she becomes very animated: "*Everything!* The teachers were ... [trails off], and the classes were smaller so it was more one on one. And it seemed like the teachers *actually cared* about their students." Speaking of one such teacher, she says,

> I remember one teacher I had. He could tell I was just down—he was my favorite—um, and you know he asked me to stay after class, 'cause I had a study hall the next period, and you know, he just asked me, "Are you *okay?* What's going on? Do you want to talk about it?" And it's like, wow! You know, thank you! So I told him all about it, and he told me if I ever needed to talk to him again, talk to him.

Although this school was a key source of support and stability for Hannah, being in foster care is anything but stable. Hannah says, "I bounced around from school to school." In the first bounce, she was taken out of the school she loved so much and reassigned to Comprehensive High. Of this period she says,

> I just couldn't suck it up and just go. I was *miserable every day* that I was there, so when I went, I hated it. I didn't go to school either, and I kinda got in trouble for that, a lot of trouble. But I could not bring myself, I didn't want to go. *I did not want to be there!*

Hannah was bounced yet again, this time to another rural school, not as small as the first but not nearly as big as Comprehensive High. When asked what she liked about it, she says, "Pretty much everything about that school. I liked the people, I liked the teachers, I liked everything." Hannah attended this school for a year, and grew both inside and outside its walls. But then she was reassigned once again to Comprehensive High. This was the determining factor in why she withdrew altogether.

> I knew I wasn't going to do well, because of the group of people that I hung out with. And once you have your reputation someplace it's really hard to change it, so people knew me as *bad kid,* and I knew I wouldn't go to school, I wouldn't, you know? So I was like, it's really not worth it. So in my eyes, I did the better thing by not going back to school and just getting my GED.

Of Comprehensive High, Hannah says simply, "it wasn't a good school for me." During our first interview, Hannah created a tangible feeling that the ultimate decision to drop out was not a choice but a matter of survival and that the key factor was the power of the *reputation* Hannah believed she had developed, a reputation that in her mind made it impossible to succeed in that environment. The reputation and its power to shape her experiences must be situated within a larger culture that is common to many public high schools: the rigid stratification of peer groups, the tensions among them, the affirmation of some groups and the denial of others by school personnel, and, in Hannah's case, a stubborn refusal to submit to disrespect.

Hannah's metaphor for Comprehensive High speaks to these social forces and offers a window into her persistent class-cutting and her eventual decision to withdraw altogether:

Hannah: [It's] one big drama whirlpool of [trails off]. I don't know [uses hands to create a whirlpool]. It was like being in prison, and it's like a competition to see who's the better person.

Jeanne: So, is that the drama, that competition between students?

Hannah: Yup.

Jeanne: Ah ha. Okay, and the whirlpool?

Hannah: It's just like all these different people thrown into one and it just creates some big, I don't know the words to explain it, but I can see it in my mind. I just can't explain it. I don't know. It's just ridiculous. I hate Comprehensive [High School].

Jeanne: So would you say you have all of these different students, um with different interests and different backgrounds, all thrown into this whirlpool together?

Hannah: It just creates chaos between one another. It's like the preppy kids don't like the punk kids and the skater kids hate the roller-bladers, cause you can tell who's obviously a skater kid, who's a punk kid, who's a prep, who's a goth. They're all labeled.

School is compulsory. Hannah had to be there whether she wanted to or not, so it felt like prison. Also like prison, it's a rigidly stratified organization. At the top of the formal power structure are administrators and teachers (or prison guards). Students (or inmates) are further down, experiencing the institution not as equals in their secondary status, but as distinct groups along a vertical continuum with differing access to informal power and prestige. And because everyone wants power and respect, their unequal distribution generates conflict and drama.

Like other young people with a stubborn sense of their own self worth, Hannah resisted being defined by others. In her relations with peers, she says,

> I got along with pretty much everybody. I didn't let anybody label me and put me into one certain group, so I kinda just got along with everybody, [except] the *rich kids*, who looked down on everybody whose parents don't own all this. They think they're better than everybody, and it really irritated me.

Hannah was much more vulnerable, however, to the institutional power of adults who had labeled her a "bad kid." In her mind, her label, her reputation, always stands in contrast to students who she believes were valued and treated better by school staff: "Oh, especially the jocks, and at [Comprehensive High] if you played sports you were golden [pause]. I didn't play sports [pause]." Simultaneously offering a critique of injustice and expressing the wound of exclusion, the final sentence is spoken so softly, and so painfully, it makes the listener ache. "I wasn't golden."

Hannah, along with her close friends, responds to the wounds of exclusion by constructing an identity outside and against privilege. During our first conversation, she makes multiple references to the "group" she hung out with and the role it played in her departure from school. During our second conversation, I ask her, "The people who were your closest friends in school, were they um, were they also feeling sort of alienated from school? Like was this a group of people you hung out with because you felt alienated?" She responds, "*Yeah, we all did!* Like that's why we used to, I think that's mainly why we used to get in a lot of trouble and cause trouble, 'cause we were trying to rebel and be like, 'Hey, f-you!' You know?"

When prompted for ways she and her peers said "F-you," she reflects,

> Oh, I've done a lot of things. It's basically just not listening to 'em. It's like, "No! You're gonna treat me like this, I'm not gonna respect you, I'm not gonna, you know, do what you want me to do. You're not gonna respect me, you're not getting *any* respect from me!" So we just wouldn't listen to 'em, and talk when we were not supposed to, and just show up late to class without a pass and not even care, or you know, not even go at all.
>
> One time I walked out of ISS [In School Suspension] 'cause she was trying to keep me, and I was like, "No! I have to go to the bathroom." And she was

like, "You have to wait." And I just picked up my stuff and I walked out. I really had to pee! [Laughs].

My friend Sarah and I—ninth period math class—we would just stroll in without a pass. I didn't care! She's not nice to us; we were not going to be nice to her. Oh, and then one time in that math class, she tried to kick me out. I'm like, "Nah, I'm not [leaving]. I'm just gonna sit here." [spoken with mock sweetness]. And she was like, "You need to GO!" And I'm like, "You know, I'm really comfortable right here." [Again, spoken with saccharin]. And Sarah's like, "Well if she's gotta get kicked out, I'm going too." So we both got kicked out of the class [laughs].

Over two years later, these memories continue to delight Hannah. But the social support she received from friends like Sarah, while essential to her day-to-day well-being, did not come without costs to her persistence in school. In retrospect, she believes that these dynamics would have prevented her from *ever* graduating, that she would still be sitting there today, not making progress, if she had remained:

I just feel like I would probably still be in high school right now, if I [stayed], because I woulda kept not doing what I was supposed to do. It's just, I guess, the group, the people I surrounded myself with woulda just been bad influences on me.

Hannah is certainly not alone in creating a peer culture that helps one get through the day, while simultaneously making it difficult to remain in school. It is within this larger context of an escalating dynamic among trouble-making, labeling, and resistance that Hannah's primary reason for leaving school—an overwhelming psychological beat down—must be situated. In the end, despite the moments of joy she experienced standing up to the adults who disrespected her, the power they ultimately had over her and the hostile environment she experienced while at Comprehensive High *wore her down.*

Like many young people who leave school early in contemporary America, Hannah had a bucket full of challenges in her life outside of school: a destructive intimate relationship, an estranged relationship with both parents, unstable foster care, and a sense of abandonment. As a child in trouble, what Hannah needed most in school were adults who cared about her *in spite of* her trouble-making behavior, adults who instead of labeling her a *bad kid* sought to find out what was going on in her life to explain her behavior, adults willing to provide the social support that is instrumental to helping adolescents get through rough times. Hannah's definition of a "perfect teacher" speaks to this:

I guess they just have to be sincere and have passion about teaching and *care* about their students. "You have a problem? Okay, I'll help you." You know, not like "humph!"—like a lot of the teachers are. So, that would be my perfect teacher. I guess some kids need people to talk to [pause], *like me* [just a whisper]. Someone who'd be willing to listen if the kid was like, "Listen, can I talk to you? I have a problem." Or say the teacher notices the kid is kind of down, one that would be like, "Are you okay?" You know, something like that, that would be a good teacher.

Hannah's experiences point to the importance of school size in the social construction and power of reputations. In very small schools, like the two Hannah attended while in foster care, faculty and staff are likely to know students quite well, warts and all. Within that context, behavior deemed unacceptable by the school has the potential to stand out more. At the same time, however, the complexity of students' larger lives is far more visible to school staff. In larger schools, reputations, like stereotypes, become shorthand ways of defining people one doesn't know as well as one should.

Hannah's story speaks powerfully of a high school stratification system that produces winners and losers, insiders and outcasts—a system that affirms the value of some kids while denying that of others. By the time Hannah was reassigned to Comprehensive High for the third time, she was a very different person than she had been at fourteen, when her out-of-school problems began. But her experiences suggested that these changes were rendered invisible by her previous reputation—"From my younger years, and I was like fifteen when I [first] left Comprehensive High. Course that's a bad age." The opportunity for young people to grow, to use their past experiences to inform their development, is overwhelmed by the static labels we attach to them when they do not conform to our expectations. Hannah was ready to move on, but she believed that the staff at Comprehensive High wouldn't let her.

Can we imagine a school system in which kids can mess up, as Hannah did and as many other kids do, and be allowed and encouraged to move ahead? In the United States, adolescence is a remarkably difficult time under the very best circumstances. Authentic thrusts toward exploration and independence are too often met with treatment befitting a very young child. Adolescents are told to "behave like an adult," but what this too often means is "comply like a child." Is it any wonder young people like Hannah feel so angry and beaten down? Hannah's story provides a powerful argument that the best school environment is one that is flexible and forgiving, one that understands that young people are not *made* but *in the making*. Such school environments do exist, but they are not typical.

$$3$$

Steve

A Gambler's Story

It's July 8, 2010, and very soon Lebron James is going to announce which NBA team he's scuttling Cleveland for. I'm sitting on the couch chatting on Facebook with a friend from graduate school and only half listening to the ESPN talking heads who are anchoring the pre-announcement media blitz. But it's clear they think he's going to Miami.

One by one, my son's closest friends show up for Lebron's press conference. They let themselves into the house and poke their heads into the living room to say hello before clomping up to Nick's room on the third floor. In one greeting after another, I say, "So, all bets are on the Heat. What do *you* think?" And echoing the earlier conversation I had with my son, each one responds with certainty, "No way!" "Really?" I ask, skeptical. With subtle variation, they offer the same narrative, and it goes like this—Why would Lebron hold a press conference to announce something so predictable (and so gutless)? That leaves two scenarios, in their view. Worst case—he affirms his allegiance to the city that has loved him so well for years. Disappointing, to be sure, but a class act none-the-less. Best case—

Canaries Reflect on the Mine, pages 25–35
Copyright © 2012 by Information Age Publishing
All rights of reproduction in any form reserved.

he commits to the Knicks and begins building a career to rival Jordan's. In either scenario, Lebron's a guy with heart and soul.

I'm not a fan of the NBA, but I am a fan of this tight circle of insistently hopeful friends, so I hope—more cautiously—along with them.

It's over. The talking heads were right, after all. Clomp—clomp—clomp—clomp. Big feet in even bigger shoes make their way down two flights of stairs. I anxiously anticipate the dark cloud hanging over them, but they are laughing. *Laughing!* The transformation from dogged optimism to mocking cynicism is seamless. One narrative hastily shrugged off, another pulled on. Lebron, honorable and scrappy one moment, a soul-less wonder the next. But the sensibilities of a Knicks fan animate both narratives. Comfort with multiple stories and unexpected outcomes allow a Knicks fan to carry on.

* * *

Stumble upon a young male in my house, and the odds are better than even you're encountering a fan of one downtrodden sports team or another. Occasionally, he'll be a card-carrying member of a trifecta of heartbreakers: Mets fan, Knicks fan, Jets fan. Steve belongs to this select group and for many years our conversations took place on the emotional landscape of love for the New York Metropolitans; one part joy, two parts exasperation. It's easy to be a Yankees fan; *that* narrative is predictable. Being a Mets fan, not so easy. You gotta believe, you gotta have heart.

Steve is sharp as a tack. He possesses an authentic magnetism fed—in almost equal parts—by wit and irreverence. He plays with language and mixes metaphors; his observations about human nature's dark side are always incisive and paradoxically heartbreaking and funny. But truth be told, I used to be a little ambivalent about his friendship with my son. Although I liked him, he struck me as a little too reckless, a bit too casual about matters of consequence.

I no longer worry about that. In fact, I've come to be especially grateful that Nick has a friend like Steve. Because here's the thing: I really didn't *know* Steve at all. In our first interview, he made this staggeringly clear. Sitting at my kitchen table, with his customary high energy—mindlessly moving the informed consent form back and forth across the table, rolling up the edges and then spreading them out again—Steve has given me a great interview. We've talked for nearly an hour. His buddies, growing impatient on the third floor, have begun texting him: *When you gonna be done?*

"Okay," I say, taking the hint, "let's finish up. Last question: What do you hope for your future?" And, completely unanticipated by either of us, a freight train of emotion rolls through my kitchen. Within a matter of seconds, the tall, athletic twenty year old becomes the grief-stricken eleven year old whose mother just left him, his three younger siblings, and his dad to fend for themselves. That was nine years ago. None of them have heard from her since. No birthday cards. No Christmas presents. No phone calls.

I've known Steve for years, but I am clueless about this singularly defining event in his life. Haltingly, I ask, "So your mom just took off?" His response—heavy, thick, and forced—elicits visions of Sisyphus:

> Yeah. Haven't talked to her. She left. It's been sixth grade, so eight, nine years maybe. When you have someone that is supposed to love you throughout all of life, and then she leaves you, what'daya do? It's the person I love the most. And then she disappeared. I mean, that probably takes part in why I dropped out too; everything [pause], everything adds up together. It's pretty intense definitely, but it makes you such a stronger person. Like anything that goes on where kids are getting stressed out, that stuff doesn't even bother me, 'cause I've already seen the worst. I can't think of anything that's worse than [throat catches, trails off].

> The thing that messes with me is you see animals, like a cat. A cat has five kittens and that cat loves those kittens. It'll never leave. It'll do anything to protect those kittens. But my mom, she left, you know what I mean? If a cat is supposedly not as intelligent as us, and they're still taking care of their kids, then why is a human being leaving their kids? It doesn't make any sense.

It doesn't make any sense. How can a child make sense of *that*? Steve embodies juxtaposition. Intellectually, he understands that things happen, things out of his control, that his mother had demons long before he was born and for which he bears no fault. Alongside this knowledge sits our culture's insistent silence about the big and small tragedies families endure. The pervasive *myth* of the ideal family where parents love their children unconditionally, sacrificing everything for them, tells Steve that there is something not right with his own family. His mother's abandonment suggests that there is something wrong with him, something shameful. Steve *is* a strong person. He thinks and acts with tenacity in an ever-shifting space between the irreconcilable. That space is the home of a gambler.

After Steve's mother left, his father was absent much of the time, struggling to keep his business afloat and his family together on his own. Steve and his siblings were often left to care for themselves. To Steve, it felt as if he had lost both parents:

The next thing you know, now that I don't have a mom, my dad's gotta work even more, and now I don't even see him at all, besides the few minutes he's home, you know what I mean. Running a business like that, you gotta be there at all times. You gotta fix machines, stuff breaks down, and when you're the only person that knows how to do stuff like that, you gotta be there and, I mean, *I respect him for doin' it,* but what it did to the family is pretty crazy. It ruined the family, and I don't want that for my family [chokes up, begins sobbing].

[My one brother] is, okay I'm twenty, [he] is nineteen, [my other brother] is eighteen, and then my sister just turned sixteen, so we're all basically pretty close in age. We're all close with each other, but you know, something's *just not right* with the whole family. 'Cause we didn't have family dinners and we didn't have social time and family picnics, 'cause you can't have that stuff when you already have a crazy business goin' on, then on top of that you got a crazy mom [choking up], and on top of that, everything is just hitting the fan at once, you know. It's a lot to take in at once, definitely. It's intense and that's why I don't wanna follow in my dad's footsteps, 'cause I've seen what it does to kids like me, I've seen what it does to kids like my brothers, my sister.

Against a backdrop of events as unpredictable as they were life-altering, Comprehensive High was a relatively stable anchor in Steve's life. An athlete and one of the "popular" kids in high school, for the most part Steve loved being there, largely for the social aspects. Of peers and the larger social environment, he says,

I had tons of friends. I mean, I had no problem making friends at school, and I don't really think anyone disliked me. There's always gonna be the kids that don't like you and the kids that maybe you don't like, but that happens everywhere. There's always gonna be cliques, there's always gonna be people hating each other. It's people. That's how people are, you know what I mean. [I had] the occasional girlfriend problems here and there, but that didn't mess up anything. Everything was good. Like I said, I loved the social aspect of high school. It's where you learn how to be a person, you know what I mean. I liked it, definitely.

Loving the social aspects of school and having made it all the way to his senior year in spite of the turmoil at home, Steve was not on a path for dropping out. His story, more than any of the others, is one of having been pushed out. As he sees it, a series of random circumstances led to his exit. A different set of circumstances could have led to his graduation. Referring to these events as "the luck of the draw," and borrowing Forrest Gump's metaphor for life, Steve says that school is:

a box of chocolates. You never know what you're gonna get, you really never do. You start out high school, everything's good. It's kinda like a roller coaster. You go up and down, you go through your times, you got your personal life goin' on, you got all your emotions running, you're going through puberty, everything's goin' crazy. Then it's like a box of chocolates. Sometimes it can mess with you, sometimes it helps you out.

This metaphor expresses Steve's larger world view and reflects a lack of predictability and control in his life. Shit happens. Shit that "doesn't make any sense." There's no rhyme or reason to it. Sometimes you get lucky, sometimes you don't. Steve's first bit of bad luck in school was an injury he sustained as a sophomore, on the lacrosse field:

I blew my knee out at one of the practices, tore my MCL, my ACL, a whole bunch of ligaments in my knee, had tons of scar tissue, had to have surgery. That took me out for at least a year and a half. I tried to come back, and my knee just wasn't holding up. And I know if I woulda stayed in sports, there's no way I was dropping out. Coach S., he's another great teacher, I love that guy, he's a motivator, you know what I mean. He keeps you goin' when you're down and out, he'll keep you going, but when injuries happen, they happen. There's nothing you can do about it.

The injury had multiple consequences. Steve, who had been playing the sport since he was eight, was not just any old lacrosse player; according to a former teammate, he was,

a feared lacrosse player. I mean, *feared*. Other teams knew of him based on how many goals he scored and how many kids he injured per game. No one could stand up to him on the field and he would just *blow through everybody*, leaving behind a broken pile of kids and lacrosse sticks.

Steve had a lot of pain to work through and he worked through a lot of it on the lacrosse field. The injury robbed him of that outlet. Moreover, while Steve loved the social aspects of school, by his own admission he was an underachiever academically. The grade requirements for sports participation motivated him to keep his academic performance at a satisfactory level; without this incentive, his academic work suffered. Perhaps most importantly, the surrogate family qualities of team membership, and especially the consistent interaction with and crucial support of Coach S., were likewise lost when Steve was injured.

In spite of this loss, Steve persisted through his sophomore and junior years of high school and was on schedule to graduate on time with mediocre grades and no surplus of credits. Steve attributes his persistence to a number of adults who "worked" with him along the way. Throughout junior high and high school, Steve was a rule breaker. Not the big rules like fighting with peers or threatening staff, but the small ones like being late, playing poker at lunch, talking in class, using his cell phone. Every administrator knew him by name. However, the consequences for these behaviors had been relatively minor because most of his teachers and especially his principal for ninth and tenth grades viewed the infractions as trivial. They had been willing to either overlook them or negotiate the consequences with Steve. Of this particular principal, Steve says,

> Oh man, he would do everything for us. He would bring us in and he would actually sit down and *talk* to the student, *like a person*, you know what I mean? He would actually *work with you*. If I was late a couple of times, first couple times, he'd let it slide, but if it was a habit then he would work with me. He wouldn't just all of a sudden throw you under the gun, and give you two Saturday detentions. He would give us two or three lunch detentions to make up for it, you know what I mean? He'd work with you, as long as you worked with him. That's what I really like about him.

Everything changed for Steve his senior year, when, in his words, he "got all the coconuts." In the first of a series of bad hands, the school administration cracked down on tardiness. Suddenly, coming to school late—something Steve had been doing for years—had real consequences. And, as (bad) luck would have it, Steve was assigned to a homeroom teacher who actually enforced the tardiness rules. In his words,

> I disliked, ah, the homeroom penalties. That's one of the reasons why I dropped out. If I was one minute late they would just give me another Saturday detention, one after another, over and over and over and over. Even when I would get there at 8:01 my homeroom teacher [would say], "Oh, you gotta go to the office and sign in." At one point I had four Saturday detentions stacked up and they wouldn't even let me get lunch detentions or work it out. That was back when I bowled on Saturdays. I'm a kid, I got stuff to do on Saturdays. But I don't know, they wouldn't even work with me on that stuff. They wouldn't negotiate anything with me. So it came to a point where I had so many detentions I was like, if I step in that school, they're gonna be on me like hotcakes, you know, they're gonna be all over me. [The principal will] be in my homeroom, coming to my first period class, coming to my second period, pullin' me out in the hallway, embarrassing me, saying "hey, you gotta serve these and oh, by the way, now you've got two in-school detentions."

It came to a point where I would just rather not go to school. Instead of being one minute late, I would just rather not go to school, 'cause then I wouldn't have to serve the Saturday detention. So if I got there at 8:02, I'd be like, oh, might as well just leave, because I'm gonna get another Saturday detention tacked on.

Skipping school to avoid Saturday detentions came at a cost; Steve found himself failing three classes he needed for graduation. Moreover, in another bad hand, these classes were taught by teachers who would not work with him. Again, he perceives this as the luck of the draw:

> Like anything else, some of the teachers really wouldn't work with you if you got back work and stuff like that. A lot of teachers will work with you, but there are a couple that won't, and there's no ifs, ands, or buts about it. And my senior year, it just so happens it was more that wouldn't help me out than would help me out. I just got so far behind that I couldn't even catch up. Some teachers—like say if you missed a day—sometimes you'd have pop [quizzes], tests out of nowhere, and they wouldn't even acknowledge it. So I'd go into school the next day, and they don't say anything, "Hey you missed a test, you gotta make that up." So a lot of times I would just get my report card thinking I would get a good grade, and what do you know, I missed two tests that they didn't even say anything about. So then, I try to go back and, "Hey can I make up this test?" and "Oh no, it's past the marking period. The grades are in. You can't do anything. There's nothing we can do. You're gonna have to do better on this next period." But then, my grade was so bad on that marking period that I couldn't even bring my grade up to a passing level, you know what I mean.

By mid-year, it was clear that Steve would not be able to graduate with his class. This came as a blow, but because Steve did not hate Comprehensive High like most of the other young people I talked with, he was willing to come back for another year. He had even worked out a plan with his guidance counselor: "I was gonna [leave school and] work for the rest of the year for my dad, and then go back to school the next year, and graduate with your son and them, and I was fine with that." Steve's father was also on board with this plan. However, when he, his dad, and his guidance counselor presented the plan to school administrators, he was dealt his final bad hand: "The principals told me 'your grades aren't good enough to go to any four-year school anyway, so right now your best option is just to get your GED and move on with your life.'" Taken aback by this account, I respond, "So, the administrators *encouraged* you to leave?" Steve answers,

> Yes! [The principal] said, "Once you get some money in your pocket and get out in the real world, that's when [kids] usually don't wanna come back and follow our rules and go back to school. Here, sign these papers!" 'Cause I had to sign release papers, and right at the end of that conversation, they were already throwing [the papers at me]. *They were pushing me right out*

> *the door.* That's how it was, when I was two, three credits away from being a graduated high school senior. It was ridiculous, it was ridiculous!
>
> They talked me into it. Being a kid, you can get manipulated, and when you got all these adults throwing these papers and telling me "just do this, just do this," I mean *being a kid—it's hard to stick up for yourself,* you know, and you got four adults telling you to drop out, and deep in my heart I wanna stay and just finish it, 'cause everyone wants to. I been through 13 years, you know what I mean, and then all of a sudden I'm a semester away, and then all this happens and now I'm not gonna graduate.
>
> *Now* I can stick up for myself, but that's three years in the *real world.* I know how a lot more stuff works now. You gotta trust your heart and you gotta trust yourself, and back then I had that, but I just didn't have the confidence to come out and say it, you know what I mean. So that's the difference between then and now. I trust myself now. Back then, I trusted myself, but I just I couldn't let it out.

It's worth comparing Steve's and Ivan's final encounters with school administrators. Ivan, figuratively speaking, had already exited the building. He was just looking for a reason, during that meeting, to get up, walk out the door, and never look back. The administrators did not disappoint him. Steve, in contrast, was looking for a way to *stay in* and was completely blindsided by the response he got. His rendering of what happened captures powerfully the pain and helplessness he felt. As he saw it, the administrators were telling him he was expendable. According to one common sense view of kids and schooling, one might ask: Why didn't Steve just get in line his senior year? If he was that close to graduating, why didn't he just do the Saturday detentions and get a good alarm clock? Where does personal responsibility come into this equation? Steve, in fact, recognizes his own role in the events leading up to the final push out the door, and faults himself for not getting with the program:

> Being 17, your priorities sometimes aren't all there. Like now, like looking back at it, I would have done everything completely different. If I had the chance, I would go back, and I'd *be* there, and I would participate so much more. You know, I hated waking up, I hated doing this, I hated doing that, I hated homework. But now, looking back, I would love to do it all again, and do it right this time, you know what I mean, but like I said, my priorities weren't that good back then.

At the same time, Steve makes it clear that "three years in the real world" brought him to this conclusion; it was not within reach while he was still in school. And he also senses that he is not singularly responsible for his outcome: "I'm not blaming anyone else for why I dropped out, but if things woulda been a little bit different then maybe everything woulda been different." In Steve's case, *a little bit different* could have made all the difference in the world. A less rigid tardy policy, a different homeroom teacher, a more flexible administrator; any one of these things could have changed Steve's high school outcome. Given Steve's biography, it's not hard to see how he interprets the series of events as a crapshoot.

However, even if these seemingly random events had not occurred, even if Steve had made it to the graduation podium, he would still have been a kid in enormous pain. More than anything, he needed someone to wonder what was going on in his life, and to care enough to find out. No one did.

> I've seen so much, it's crazy, but like the principals and everybody, they don't know that. Nobody knows any of this stuff. It just woulda been nice if people were there to help me along the way. In elementary they were, they were there, but come high school, I don't know if it's just too many kids and they can't help people, but I just never got any [help], no help at all. And when you got stuff like that goin' on in your personal life, high school is like your second life, you know what I mean? It's not your top priority. I'm basically growing up on my own, and that's how high school was. It's really intense, it's just being a kid, goin' through stuff like that is too much, way too much, and when you got no one to fall back to, it makes it even harder. You just have yourself.

In *The Road to Whatever*, Elliot Currie (2004) tells the stories of white, middle class adolescents in trouble. Based on in-depth interviews and observations with young people, Currie paints a vivid and deeply troubling picture of American society and its schools, one that resonates with the experiences of several young people in this study, including Steve. Describing the school experiences of the young people he talked with, Currie (2004) writes:

> With few exceptions, the school's role was less an active, nurturing, capacity-building one than a passively monitoring one, a sorting of students into appropriate piles rather than a concerted effort to bring all of them up to their best potential. And this conception of the school's role fits seamlessly into the larger culture of passive individualism in which the schools were embedded. If it is seen as being up to the individual, even as a child, to rise and fall on his or her own, then the responsibility of the school is less to help children than to simply measure how far they go—to classify them according to how well they meet, or how dismally they fail to meet, conventional standards of social and intellectual performance and to declare them officially out of the race if they fail badly enough. (p. 7)

This depersonalized and passive stance is consistent with Steve's perception that, in twelfth grade, his teachers and administrators were indifferent to his problems:

> It's all there, all through elementary I was in counseling, so there's obviously files somewhere about that. If they cared just a little bit to look into it they woulda known all of it. But obviously they didn't care enough, so they didn't look into it once.

Steve interpreted this indifference as an assessment of him as a person, a person unworthy of support: "[They] bring up your records on the computer and say 'Okay, you have 30 detentions. Okay, you been late. Okay this teacher left you a comment saying you're a *bad person*, you talk in class.'" Of the principal who encouraged him to leave, Steve says, "[He would] look down upon you all the time, you know what I mean? He'll just make you feel like you're the bottom of the pile, you're just trash." For someone like Steve, struggling with a profound sense of abandonment and wondering at some deep level if it's his fault, acquiescing to such treatment is like agreeing that he's a bad person. In self-preservation mode, Steve refused:

> If you're trying to sit down and talk to a principal that has completely shit on you the whole time that you've been there, it's kinda hard to even take in anything they're saying, 'cause at that point you're just fed up with it. They just go on about their business and do what they do, you know, and I guess they're doing their jobs, but at the same point they aren't doin' their jobs, 'cause their job's to keep everybody in that school, and not push them out, you know what I mean.

In a different world, keeping everyone in school would be the job of a principal. In this world, Steve and other students who don't fit the mold are seen as excess baggage. As Steve says, "They give you one choice, and if you don't want that choice, then 'See ya!'" Again, this is consistent with Currie's (2004) findings:

> Children's problems at school—especially if they involved a challenge to the authority of teachers or principals—were regarded as evidence of fundamental flaws of character, which called not for assistance but exclusion. Youth with behavior problems were seen less as children in need than as enemies to be put outside the gates, and what happened to them then was not of great moment. (p. 202)

Steve's departure from Comprehensive High was of no great moment for his principal; in fact, it meant he had one fewer student to monitor and discipline. His days were probably a little bit easier with Steve gone. Leaving school from Steve's perspective, in contrast, was *monumental*. Echoing Ivan's assertion that "only fucking losers drop out of high school," Steve describes the worst thing about dropping out:

> The worst thing? The nightmares! You have nightmares. In your mind, it must be always in the back of your head—"*I'm a failure.*" You know what I mean? You'll have these crazy dreams about graduating high school and everything's going good. Blah, blah, blah, blah. And then you'll wake up, and then *you're a failure.* You wake up and, "Oh wait! I didn't graduate. I didn't *even* graduate from high school. *I'm worthless!*" That's the worst thing about [dropping out]. It's just always in the back of your head—hey what woulda happened if I woulda graduated and went to college and done everything different? It's just the "what if?" The "what if?" question is the worst part about it, and that's the 100 percent honest [truth]. That's what has been bothering me. But I mean at the same time you just gotta move on, you made your decisions, there's nothing you can do, you just gotta keep goin'.

And Steve has kept on going. These days, he's gambling. And he's *really* good at it. Gambling professionally is not for the faint of heart. Winning big demands an uncommon comfort with risk and a steely confidence in one's ability to survive losses. Steve is well versed in big losses, and he's still standing.

To the degree that high schools shore up the students who need it the least, students who have faced minimal adversity, students whose lives have rarely put them out on a limb, our schools fail everyone. What if Steve had access to adults at Comprehensive High who knew and cared for him and had been able to channel the grit and determination he exhibited on the lacrosse field to other areas of his schooling? Can we imagine schools that not only value the tenacity and courage of students like Steve, but also employ their hard-won sensibilities to teach students whose lives have treated them more gently? How might this enrich—and transform—all students? Embodying juxtaposition, students like Steve offer windows into how far our schools are from meeting the needs of all students who pass through them, as well as models for how to persist against great odds. Gambling is one expression of this juxtaposition. Can we imagine others?

4

Adel

Refusing to be Left Behind

When I first meet Adel at the Youth Center, she's eighteen, and has been out of school for a year and a half. She's wearing jeans, a raspberry colored turtleneck, a white nylon winter vest with faux fur around the collar, and fashionable black rimmed glasses with pink accents. Her hair, pulled back into a pony tail, frames a face the rich warm color of café au lait. Unlike Hannah and Iris, who loosen up quickly and become increasingly animated as our conversations progress, Adel has a decidedly no-nonsense demeanor from the beginning to the end of this first interview. I ask *many* follow-up questions, which she answers politely, but with few details. She's not *un*friendly, but we are strangers at the start, and not a lot more familiar when we're done. Four months later, when I've finished the first draft of her story, I drop it off at her house and arrange a date for a second interview.

A week after that, I sit on my front porch anxiously waiting for her to arrive. I'm anticipating the same reserved demeanor and want to be able to greet her right away. But to my delight, something has *shifted*. She gets

Canaries Reflect on the Mine, pages 37–45
Copyright © 2012 by Information Age Publishing
All rights of reproduction in any form reserved.

out of her car with a big smile, crosses the street and bounds up my steps. A few minutes later, she's sitting at my kitchen table telling me that she's registered for classes at my college, and that she's *so* excited to start. We look over her schedule, and I make some recommendations for dropping certain classes and adding others. Although I don't know her as well as I'd like, I have a sense about the kinds of teachers and pedagogies that would support her needs as a learner. A few of the classes I'd like to see her in are full, so I make some phone calls to colleagues who agree to let her enroll. Then we begin discussing her story. I'm encouraged when she tells me that after she read it, she gave it to her mother to read. And I'm more than a little surprised when she says they both think I got it right, or right enough that she is now more willing to add nuance and detail.

Unlike Iris and Isabel, Adel's experiences with peers were largely positive. She had lots of friends and, like Steve, loved the social aspects of school. I ask, "Alright, think about the kids at school, your peers at school, were there any that you really liked? That you really liked spending time with?" "Yeah," she says, "pretty much *everybody in my class,* my graduating class, I got along with pretty much all of them." "So you didn't have a particular group that you hung out with?" I ask. "Not really," she says. "It was a little bit of everybody, I was mixed in with everybody." The only peers she says she didn't like were upper classman, who "thought because they were [older] they could control everything." Adel's sense of connection with her classmates, her *identity* as a member of her graduating class, is the context for her decision to drop out at the end of eleventh grade when it became clear she had no hope of graduating on time. She would not be able to walk to the podium with her classmates. She would be left behind while her friends moved on:

> I just didn't wanna be the only one—like out of my friends—still in school, when they've all graduated. I just kept thinking, "*Oh my god! All my friends are graduating next year! I'm not gonna graduate with my friends!*" So I just stopped going.

Although the relationship between grade retention and dropping out of school has been well documented (Rumberger, 1995, 2004), less attention has been paid to what this *feels* like from the perspective of students like Adel. Advocates of retention neglect the existential experience of being "held back." In treating learning as a solitary and discrete process, rather than as an act of "communion" (Noddings, 2005, p. 36), they fail to recognize that children and young people are not likely to learn the curriculum the second—or third—time around any better in the absence of friends and a sense of belonging. Adel's need to be with her friends is one of the strongest messages to come out of our conversations.

So, the primary reason Adel dropped out was because she could not graduate with her friends, but her journey to this point tells multiple stories about the structure of schooling. The surface obstacle to graduating on time, for Adel, was ninth grade English. As an eleventh grader, Adel was taking English Nine for the third time and had no hope of completing the required English Language Arts units by the time her friends would graduate. She was doing reasonably well in all her other classes, and very well in math, for which she says she has a natural affinity. But her history with English was rocky, and for different reasons she missed a ton of these classes as a freshman and sophomore. The first time she failed English Nine, she was assigned to a first period class. Like Steve and Ivan, who rarely made it to school for first period, Adel often slept through English. In her words, "Like my first year [in English Nine] it wasn't that I didn't get English, but it was the first period of the day, and I was always late to school, because I'm not a morning person."

A moment to pause and consider is necessary. A close friend of mine, Darlene Gold, read an earlier version of Adel's story. Another close friend, Phil Tate, read an early draft of Steve's. Their reactions were nearly identical; both were a little miffed that these young people couldn't seem to get themselves out of bed in the morning. In the margins of Steve's story, Phil scribbled, "Why didn't he just buy a good alarm clock?" Of Adel, Darlene wrote,

> The bit about "not being a morning person" feels incomplete for me. As I read that line I wondered how much schools would have to change to accommodate each person's constantly shifting set of needs & preferences. Forgive me, but it almost seemed bratty: like it was too inconvenient to attend school, and yet somehow that's the school's fault for starting too early. I guess I can't help wonder why it was too hard to get to school for that first period class. (personal communication, February 12, 2011)

Phil and Darlene's reactions revealed a tacit assumption in my analysis; doesn't everyone know that the sleep patterns of adolescents are different than young children and adults? Apparently not. Considerable research on adolescent sleep, school start times, and academic performance provides evidence that Adel, Steve, and Ivan are not uncommon (Eaton et al., 2010; Georgios, Millrood, & Mateika, 2002; Randler & Frech, 2009; Wolfson & Carskadon, 2003, 2005; Yan & Slagle, 2006). According to Wolfson and Carskadon (2005),

Our data indicate that, at least as far back as 1986, the majority of the high schools started too early in the morning for most adolescents' sleep needs and schedules, as well as daytime functioning. Many high-school and middle-level students cannot get to sleep early due to a combination of biological and psychosocial factors. (p. 51; see also Fischer et al., 2008)

Many people operate on a common sense assumption that goes like this: In the "real world," people have to get up in the morning. Schools *cannot* accommodate a multitude of sleep patterns, and more importantly, they *should not* accommodate them, because young people need to get ready for the "real world." While there is a certain—capitalist—logic to this argument (Bowles & Gintis, 1977), it challenges two interrelated values associated with public schooling. The first is learning. The research suggests that even if Adel, Steve, and Ivan had never missed a first period class, they would not have been operating on all cylinders; their learning would have been compromised. Second, this argument challenges equality of educational opportunity in a number of ways. Since some young people can and do function well early in the morning, they will learn better based not on effort, but rather on their bio-rhythms. Randler and Frech (2009) found that early risers performed better in school and had higher academic achievement. If you add to this the vastly different out-of-school responsibilities of young people in upper and lower classes, those who must hold a job, care for siblings, or otherwise support their families' day-to-day survival are further penalized. Additionally, students who, like Iris, Isabel, David, and Adel, struggle with traditional *in school* learning must devote more time *out* of school to homework, which can further undermine their sleep and overall functioning. And, finally, young people like Steve, Ivan, and Adel, who come to school late, not only miss classroom learning, they are also punished for their tardiness with lunch detentions, after school detentions, and in the worst case, Saturday detentions. Punitive responses such as these are also correlated with dropping out.

So, although it would be inconvenient and bureaucratically challenging, a commitment to high quality learning for all would require "a variety of school schedule options that will benefit adolescents' sleep and daytime functioning needs" (Wolfson & Carskadon, 2005, p. 49). On a somewhat tangential note, Wolfson and Carskadon (2005) found that "of schools changing or contemplating a high school schedule change, 55% cited athletic practices as a major barrier" (p. 49). In fact, the negative impact on school sports was cited more frequently than any other barrier (e.g., transportation challenges, teacher reluctance, community opposition), lending support to the perception of several young people in this study that athletes are more highly valued than other students.

In short, Adel failed English Nine the first time because she couldn't get up that early in the morning. Because all students are required to complete the equivalent of four full years of English Language Arts instruction, Adel's failure of English Nine the second time sealed her fate.[1] Her second time around, she was in a class of strangers instead of friends, and a poor relationship with her teacher that became increasingly more hostile over time led eventually to her refusal to attend class: "I had [this teacher] and I just didn't want to go to his class because I didn't like him." Probed for why this was, Adel responds,

> I don't know, he just seemed really rude. And I understand that kids shouldn't be late, but when you're coming from all the way downstairs, from the cafeteria to get all the way upstairs, it's packed, there's kids going to lunch, and then kids coming from lunch, too. *You're not the only one.* And [you need to stop] at your locker. And he just always yelled at you right when you got in the classroom if you were late, even if you were only like a minute late, he'd yell, and just was really strict.

Strict and *rude* are two adjectives that Adel uses repeatedly to describe school staff she dislikes. When asked to share some things that these staff did, in order to describe what she means by strict, she says: "[They] just always seemed to be rude. Yelling. Not really caring about the reason why you're late, not understanding about it. Just rude. They seem to have like a negative vibe toward everything." Two critiques stand out in Adel's description, and also permeate much of her narrative about teachers. "Not really caring about the reason why you're late, not understanding about it," speaks to a desire, expressed repeatedly by many of these young people, for teachers who were willing to step into their shoes and consider their contexts. Comprehensive High is a physically large and architecturally challenging building. Although the junior high classes are located in one area, once a student enters ninth grade, her classes can be located anywhere within this monolith of a building. The amount of time students are given to move from one class to the next, often times needing to go to their lockers or the bathroom, is a meager three minutes. If, as is the case in some European countries, high school students remained in homeroom for all of their classes while their teachers moved from one class to the next, I suspect that transition times would, as they are in these countries, be more generous.

Adel's second critique speaks more generally to the *golden rule.* Like Hannah, Adel is not one to submit passively to disrespect. And, like Hannah, Adel's story illustrates the unequal power of students and teachers: a dance of teacher disrespect and student push back that escalates over time. Adel describes this poignantly,

I understand that there's rules and all that, but I don't like to be told what to do all the time, and yelled at, and I guess you could say I have a bad temper. If someone yells at me, I tend to yell back, and that got me in a lot of trouble. And then it just seemed like after one referral, I was getting another one and another one, because of my attitude and the way I was talking. But it was also because I didn't like the way people were talking to me. And I guess, I stood up for myself.

Also like Hannah, Isabel, and Iris, Adel contrasts the treatment she received with that of other, more favored, students. She remarks, "Teachers have to have positive attitudes towards *all* kids, not just *certain* ones." When I ask who got the positive treatment, she says,

Oh it seemed like [students] that already knew what was going on, what the topic was about, [teachers] seemed to just really click with them ones, and the ones that didn't [know what was going on], [teachers] didn't really seem like they wanted to help them.

"And what is the experience for the student that doesn't know what's going on?" I ask,

[You're] sittin' there, you're just dozing off, drawing, and then your hand starts hurting, and then you're not really paying attention 'cause you're not understanding it, and it just seems boring *because you don't understand it!* I understood math, so it didn't matter which way he did it, any of the teachers did it, I could pick up on it.

This particular narrative is about exclusion and neglect, being supported or being ignored. But later Adel makes it clear that she's experiencing a more active assault than the term neglect implies. Through her eyes, her lack of competence with English results in less rather than more academic support from the teacher, who simultaneously communicates a "vibe" that says some students are more worthy than others. The stakes are much higher than a bad grade. Within a context of neglect and disrespect, Adel is asked to make her lack of competence *visible* to everyone. Simply being *present* in this class is an invitation to the ongoing stress of public humiliation:

I don't write essays good. And I hated it! It was always "write an essay on this," "write a paragraph on this." "Read this book and write a page about it." I'm not a good writer. And I just don't like to. And then with standing up in front of the classes, it just made it hard. 'Cause if you said a word wrong, you got all these people just looking at you and you feel embarrassed.

Is it any wonder that she skips this class, that she says, very simply, "I didn't feel the need to go to class anymore." In contexts such as these, students like Adel face a no-win situation: they can remain in class without learning and always in danger of public humiliation, or they can withdraw entirely. What would you do?

Like Iris, skipping the bad class eventually spills over to other classes as well. By the time Adel officially withdrew from school at the end of eleventh grade, she had missed two full months, was failing everything, and had reached the same conclusion as Isabel and Iris: "I just feel at the high school they don't, they really don't care if you graduate." And once she had concluded that "they really don't care" she decided that school is "nothing I [want] to do."

Adel also tells other stories, lovely stories, of three teachers in high school. These stand as a counter-narrative for schooling. Like all of the young people who talked with me, the teachers Adel remembers with affection were those who were generous with their time, and consistently communicated that they cared for and valued her. One teacher she describes accordingly:

> If you needed help with something, he didn't, I don't know, make you feel embarrassed to wanna ask a question about it. And he just seemed like an overall nice person in general, so it just made class a lot more fun. I used to go, "Oh yeah, I'm going to this class!" 'Cause he's not rude and when you want help he helps you, and he gives you his free periods when you can come in and work on things.

Another teacher, Adel describes as "actually there" as opposed to physically present. When I ask what she means by this, she says,

> It didn't seem like she was just *there* to teach to get paid. It was that she wanted *every one of her students* to pass, and to *become something*, and like obviously she knew that it was my third year in English. She made sure I was going to my English lab, made sure I was getting my work done, made sure I understood something, gave me the time if I did miss school, gave me the time to make up my work, and asked if I needed any help with it.

Contrary to conventional wisdom about students who struggle with traditional classroom learning, Adel welcomed intellectual challenge and the opportunity to both make sense of and share what she was learning. Two of these three teachers engaged her in active and deep learning, as opposed to wide coverage and recall.

We had to do PowerPoints, and then we presented them to the class, and then presenting them in her class didn't make me feel like I was [pause] dumb. We had time to research it, and then put the project together, and then present it to the class. And that way the class would know what we were talking about, 'cause we had like the same mind frame. If it was grammar, it was pretty much all of us would pick pronouns or something like that, and then one person [would] just work on *one* thing, or a group of kids work on that *one* thing, and then make a PowerPoint on what it is, tell you, give you different examples, and if you have somebody around thinking the same way you are, telling you it, then all of the kids are gonna understand it.

This is a classroom characterized by what Giroux (2003) refers to as *public time*, which "slows time down ... [and] fosters dialogue, thoughtfulness, and critical exchange" (p. 149). Adel's description of this pedagogy speaks not only to Giroux's concept, but offers a remarkable insight. When students are asked to perform the more demanding work of *making meaning*, instead of regurgitating information, normative academic skills—skills that often have more to do with outside social and cultural capital than with inside school learning—count for less. The playing field becomes more level. Of a science teacher, she offers a similar description of public time's focus and depth:

He had us work on a certain topic and then present it to the class, because we would put it in a way that kids our age would understand it. And then we'd get the concept and pass. 'Cause, like you just had a different topic, and we worked on *just that topic*. At the end we all presented our topics to each other, and it just made it easier for us all to understand.

Remembering the anxiety she expressed about standing in front of her ninth grade English class, I ask Adel what was different about presenting in this science class. She describes a classroom space where students are encouraged to collaborate and care for one another, a supportive community purposefully created by her teacher:

Jeanne: Now when you did presentations for Mr. G., that was comfortable?

Adel: Yeah, 'cause like he gave you time to, I don't know, *connect* with all the kids I guess you could say.

Jeanne: So you felt like people were rooting for you?

Adel: Yeah!

Jeanne: Like everybody was just kind of, everybody wanted everybody to do well?

Adel: Yeah, not like English. Like English you got a lot of people who can read and write really good, and you got people that can't, and then with science you've got all these different terms that a lot of people don't know, so you're not afraid to mess up. You're not afraid to say a word wrong. And like Mr. G., he was like *standing right next to you, helping you* with the word if you didn't understand it.

He "was standing right next to you" speaks to a relationship between equals, reflecting the pedagogical practice Freire (1970) refers to as *dialogue*. Adel, Cole, Hannah, and Steve all characterized the teachers they loved as ones who treated them as equals, as friends. In such a relationship, the partners give and take, reflect on each other's needs, and make adjustments in order to foster communication and growth. This idea is expressed in the following exchange:

Jeanne: Okay, now if you think about the two of them together, Mr. G. and Mr. R., were there any qualities that they had in common? Like you'd say, they were both . . .

Adel: They were both [pause]—they never gave up. They tried to act like they were, like they were one of us, and help us out.

Jeanne: So when you say "one of you," you mean not above you?

Adel: Yeah.

Jeanne: Yeah, okay.

Adel: Like another student.

Jeanne: Um hum.

Adel: And if we didn't get something, they'd explain it in a different way, trying to get us to understand it. They wouldn't just give up after one time.

In the juxtaposition of what she most loved and most hated about schooling, Adel articulates the rich and wonderful possibilities of learning in a context based on respect for students, time to engage deeply and to make meaning, opportunities to work with rather than against peers, and genuine dialogue among all participants. Do these ideas strike you as outrageous? Do they speak only to the needs of struggling students? Or do they resonate with all learners? If you were given a choice to learn in any of the classes she describes, which would you choose?

5

Cole

Making Money, Making Sense

S tanding a lanky six feet tall, eighteen year old Cole has bright blue eyes and strawberry blond hair, cut very short. In grey hoodie and jeans, he greets me with a confident handshake and a wide smile. He possesses an uncommon ease with adults. Cole's personal biography, including a turbulent family life and multiple moves, combined with his sharp intellect have given way to a young person who is profoundly self-reliant and socially savvy. Cole learned at a young age that he needed to fend for himself, and he's been remarkably successful at doing so for years.

Cole came to Comprehensive High as a "new kid" in eleventh grade. In spite of entering a milieu with already established groups, Cole had no problem making friends:

> I ended up hanging out with the skateboarding crowd. 'Cause I'm a skateboarder and that's what I did for most of my life—was skateboard. So I ended up hanging out with them and got along with them just fine.

Canaries Reflect on the Mine, pages 47–51
Copyright © 2012 by Information Age Publishing
All rights of reproduction in any form reserved.

Cole attributes his ability to "fit right in" not only to the friendship extended by fellow skaters, but to his own history of school movement. By the time Cole enrolled at Comprehensive High, he had "been to plenty of other schools." He remarks, "I lived in Florida, so I went to Northport High School, Sarasota High School, Calis Park High School, Jefferson High School, so I've been to a lot of other high schools."

Unlike young people who have lived in the same community their whole lives, Cole has observed peer relationships and hierarchies in multiple schools, and can step back and analyze patterns, such as the informal power of the "sports type students." Cole characterizes this group: "Like, 'oh, I'm good at sports, so I can get on you or get on somebody else.'" Rather than feeling insecure or defensive in relation to this group, he rationalizes their behavior: "Basically they got a big ego, and they were trying to fill it." Armed with a bigger-picture understanding of peer dynamics, Cole has adopted a more philosophical and less personal perspective: "There's groups, like there's a popular group, there's an unpopular group, they all sit at different tables during lunch, and there's some groups you don't even bother talking to." For Cole, this is simply a matter of fact, not a reason to lose sleep. He uses his wide repertoire of experiences to develop and refine his social skills among peers and some adults as well. Cole, the new kid, recruited more youth for this study than any of the other participants, suggesting membership in a social web that extends beyond that of many young people who have lived here their whole lives.

Describing himself as a straight-A student up until seventh grade, Cole says he would never have dropped out of school had his home life been different. In a conversation with Susan, the assistant director of the local youth center, Cole said that he believed that most kids drop out because of problems at home, not what's going on in school. This perception was echoed in his interview with me when I asked him what was missing in my questions. He said,

> I think it's a lot on what goes on at home, has a lot to do with it. That's one thing that I didn't think you asked. I was—my parents were split up—I was moving, once a year. I went to a different school every year of my life. Um, if you have [pause], if your parents are doing certain activities, and you know what it is, you know what's happening, and you don't wanna be around it, so you just try to get away from it. That's what I did. When I was 13, I started moving in with my friends, just to get away from that. So I was a straight-A student all the way up to seventh grade, and that's when I started actually knowing what's going on in life, was about then.

Cole's belief that problems at home are a contributing factor in dropout decisions finds support in the literature. Rumberger, for instance, found a correlation between "broken homes" and dropping out (1995). Lessard et al. (2008), found that "family turmoil" is one among several factors that "set the stage" for dropping out (p. 31). But their research also suggests that a stage set is not a fait accompli. Other factors, factors operating in schools themselves, can work to either "prolong" or "sabotage" school persistence (Lessard et al., 2008). It's crucial to identify school factors that are pliable, because, as Lee and Breen (2007) argue, the contemporary context of family life makes many adolescents more reliant on school contexts to support their healthy development. Cole is one among many young people who cannot depend on family as a reliable source of social support. Schools, however, have young people for six-plus hours a day, five days a week. A lot of social support can be offered in that time.

Cole's experiences both in and out of school suggest that two types of interconnected social supports could have made a difference for him: close relationships with caring adults and respect for and responsiveness to his particular circumstances. Like a number of the young people who told me their stories, when Cole was asked what he would change about schooling if he was "king for a day," without hesitation he said,

> Smaller classes. Smaller classes would be probably the biggest change, 'cause I think it's easier to learn when you have a smaller group. It's easier for the teacher to teach 'em, they can work with 'em one on one more time than they would with a class of 30. So that'd probably be one of the biggest changes.

Cole's description of the one high school he really liked illustrates this theme further:

> There's only a few schools that I liked. I've been in and out of school, and one of the schools that I liked the most was my "second chance" school that I went to, 'cause there was under ten people in the classroom, so the teacher could work with you individually, and I loved it! I went to school every day there, and I wouldn't miss a day, 'cause I enjoyed going there. I mean the teachers got along with you great. Like I had a teacher, we called him B; he didn't care if we called him by his last name. B, that was good enough for him. So I mean he got [to be] like one of your friends, and he would still teach you. I liked that.

Like Hannah and Steve, Cole was not a struggling learner and did not have a need for academic assistance. His desire for smaller classes and individualized attention speaks more to the need for adult social support to help with the crises he was dealing with outside of school. He needed a connection to adults that would extend beyond the traditional teacher-student relationship. The traditional relationship too often sets the student and teacher in opposition, distancing them when what is most needed is closeness. Describing two teachers he did connect with at Comprehensive High, he says,

> They were just cool. They knew what was going on, they were down to earth, they thought like you would think, and they'd just *use* it, and talk to you normally, not like a teacher, but talk to you like a friend. That's what I liked.

By knowing *what was going on*, by empathizing, by offering friendship, these adults communicated not only that they cared, but also that they understood Cole had a larger life that couldn't be neatly disposed of when he entered the classroom.

Respecting Cole's larger life and recognizing and responding to his particular strengths is the second type of social support Cole needed. Cole needed to be treated like an adult. For a young person who has persevered under very difficult home circumstances since the age of 13, a young person who has already developed a level of street smarts and adult wisdom far beyond his years, being treated like a little kid was a recipe for Cole's rejection of school altogether. His metaphor for school expresses the contradiction of having to live like an adult outside of school while being treated like a child within its walls:

> School reminds me of—like I'm not saying I've ever been to one, but I've been visiting—*a minimum security penitentiary*. You're basically there from time to time, you have to follow every rule, you can't dress the way you wanna dress, there's so many codes. It's just, you don't have a lot of freedom over yourself while you're in school. [At Comprehensive High] you're always getting in trouble for something, no matter what, if you're not doing anything wrong, you're getting in trouble for something. You'll be sitting at lunch talking amongst your friends, and they'll hear something and just come over and start saying something about what they heard. I don't like that they just jump right into your business.

Cole's time at Comprehensive High lasted only half a school year; he dropped out at the age of 17, in eleventh grade. By the time he had reached Comprehensive High, his connection to formal schooling was so tenuous that a Herculean effort on the part of school personnel would have been required to keep him there. His actual experience confirmed for him that additional time in high school was going to add nothing of value to his life, and a lucrative job opportunity was more than enough to pull him away.

> Well, I was offered a job in Oklahoma, hanging garage doors, making pretty good money, so that was pretty much the main decision that made me do it. I wasn't [pause] I was already not going to school. I wasn't likin' it, so pretty much one of my friends called me one day and told me he moved out to Oklahoma and he's working for Overhead Door, can get me a job there, and I could move out of my house, and go out on my own. So I took advantage of it and I went and did it, and I stayed out in Oklahoma for almost a year, and then came back here.

Whereas school offered nothing of value in Cole's eyes, the job offered not only *pretty good money*, but also the opportunity to further develop his independence: "I moved out on my own, and I learned how to survive on my own. That's probably the best thing [about dropping out]." In fact, given the realities of Cole's life, learning to survive on his own was of far greater value than formal school learning.

It may be true that Cole's journey to dropping out was so far underway that nothing could have been done at Comprehensive High to turn the ship around. What is clear, however, is that not getting to know him and his particular needs added fuel to the ship, supporting the path it was already on. Perhaps because Cole has developed so many real life survival skills along the way, skills that serve him every day in areas where the high school valedictorian would likely flounder, he expresses no remorse about his decision to drop out. The worst thing about it, he says, was "having to go back a year later and take a test just to get the diploma. That's probably the worst thing, and that's not even that bad." I prompt, "So there aren't any *big* bad things about having dropped out?" He responds, "Not really."

6

Isabel

"I pretty much felt like I wasn't even there"

It's an overcast day in February. The windows of the conference room at the Youth Center look out on a parking lot full of dirty snow, oily puddles, and salt covered cars. The scene is bleak. There is nothing inviting about it. Feeling the cold, Isabel never removes her white puffy winter coat. But she, herself, offers a stunning contrast to the austere-looking world outside those windows. Her deep brown eyes are pools of warmth. Her light brown hair is pulled neatly back into a partial pony tail made up of a series of smaller, intricately constructed pony tails; it's a cheerful look. Her smile is genuine, but tentative. She's twenty years old and has been out of school for about three years. I've recently interviewed her younger brother David, and perhaps because of that, she has anticipated my questions. She's given a lot of thought to her experiences at Comprehensive High, to her decision to leave, and to what this means for her present and future. At seven months pregnant with her first child, a daughter, her hopes for this child are central in her mind as she shares her story:

> I just hope the schools get better 'cause I have a daughter on the way in. I really don't want [long pause], I've been almost *afraid* to have her go to Comprehensive Schools, 'cause of things I went through. I just hope there's a way that it can get better and the teachers and stuff can all be more helpful, maybe.

Isabel is a truly *sweet* young woman. She's caring to the core and remains cautiously hopeful that others will extend care to her, in spite of many experiences that defy such hope. Isabel's sense of herself in relation to others and her dreams for her future speak powerfully to this essential kindness and to why she left school in the first place:

> [My hopes for the future?] That's easy. I wanna finish going through this EDP program and getting my high school diploma. And I wanna go take classes, child development classes or classes to become a teacher. I just don't like being the kind of person that's *always mean* to people or not willing to help *certain* people. I've wanted to always be a teacher or even do daycare or have my own foster home so therefore I could help kids and teach them things that I didn't get taught, and get the education they need.

In a heartbreakingly matter-of-fact way, Isabel renders a story of educational neglect and peer victimization, frankly exposing her vulnerabilities. She says she struggled all through school, but felt especially on her own once she entered ninth grade:

> Pretty much it's been the same all through elementary school, but as I did get into the high school a lot of it did get a lot harder, and I felt like, I knew I *could* do it, but I had to have *that person* or *that teacher*, whatever, there to make sure if I didn't understand it, that I knew somebody else could *help* me understand it. And I didn't feel I had all that much help going into high school.

Isabel was two years behind her class when she dropped out in tenth grade, at the age of seventeen. Her story is one of repeatedly struggling alone, without *that person* or *that teacher* she needed to help her. This is the primary reason she gives for the decision to drop out. It comes up not only when asked to name her reasons for dropping out, but again and again in responses to other questions, such as what she liked most and least about school, and what changes she would make to keep students in school.

Isabel wanted, needed, and was ultimately denied three interrelated types of social support in high school. The first was individualized attention to her specific learning needs. Due to Isabel's academic difficulties and low test scores, she was assigned to Academic Intervention Services (AIS) labs for certain subjects. These labs are supposed to provide the additional support struggling students need. But even here mass instruction (Gatto, 2009) prevailed, as the following exchange makes clear.

Jeanne: Okay, before you were talking about feeling like you didn't get the help that you needed. Can you tell me a little bit more about that, like what kind of help you wanted and what were you not getting?

Isabel: Um, well there's a lot of areas in different subjects that I needed help in, like some math and stuff like that, and if I'd ask for it, they weren't really *specific*. They didn't really exactly show me exactly how it was supposed to be *done*, or even could possibly write out notes or examples of things.

Jeanne: So did you have some labs in math that you went to where you were supposed to get this extra assistance?

Isabel: Yes.

Jeanne: And even in those labs that were supposed to be about helping you [yeah], you didn't really feel like you were getting that?

Isabel: No.

Jeanne: So what did those teachers do?

Isabel: They pretty much, they were supposed to sit there and help the individuals by themselves and stuff like that, and pretty much I didn't feel they were doing that. They were helping all of us at one time, but they weren't helping specific people on specific things like I needed.

Jeanne: Okay, so it was kinda like a regular classroom [Yes] instead of devoted to the individual needs [Yes] of each student. Okay.

A second type of social support Isabel needed was to be recognized and valued within the classroom. Instead of feeling like a full-fledged member of her classes (Goodenow, 1993), she tells a story of too often sitting on the sidelines, watching vicariously as a spectator (Mills, 1959), while other students—more favored students—received support that was withheld from her:

Jeanne: Were there any teachers that you particularly didn't like or that you didn't feel that you could go to if you were having difficulty?

Isabel: Um, I can't remember half of my teachers. It's not so much that I didn't like my other teachers, it's just I didn't feel that I could go up to them and get the help I needed, 'cause they kinda had like some students I felt like were more teacher pets, like if *they* needed something it was [pause] *bam* right there for them.

Jeanne: Um hum. So are you saying you didn't feel like you were valued as highly?

Isabel: Yes!

Jeanne: Among some teachers as some other students were?

Isabel: Yes.

Jeanne: Yes, okay, okay. Um, can you think of any examples of things that any of those teachers did that sort of communicated to you that these other students were more important or more valuable?

Isabel: [pause] Well there was a couple of times, I don't remember who the teacher was, but it was English class. I had asked a couple of times about—'cause we were reading a certain book—and I would ask a couple of times about what certain words or certain meanings exactly meant, 'cause I couldn't understand them myself. And I would raise my hand or ask, and it's like they would ignore me, and then if somebody else had asked they went over and would help them out, so it was like *I pretty much felt I wasn't even there.*

Jeanne: So you felt kinda invisible.

Isabel: Yeah.

Given Isabel's real need for learning support, and her experience of neglect in this regard, she fell significantly behind her peers, making her especially vulnerable to humiliation in competitively organized classrooms. Not surprisingly then, the third type of social support Isabel desired was a safe environment where making mistakes and being "wrong" are seen as normal and necessary parts of learning, rather than as a cause for shame. This emerges during Isabel's discussion of the two teachers in junior high who did attend to her needs and who in doing so provided a safe environment for learning:

Jeanne: When I asked you what you liked about Comprehensive High, you said there were some nice teachers or some teachers that you liked?

Isabel: Yes.

Jeanne: Who were they?

Isabel: There was this one teacher in seventh grade, Mr. B., my social studies teacher, and social studies and science—I also had Mr. T. for science—those are, I wanna say, my weakest subjects, but they made it fun and more interesting than just reading out of a text-book or doing paperwork.

Jeanne: So you are now the third student to identify Mr. B. and Mr. T.

Isabel: [Laughs, and with real joy in her voice says] They're the best teachers!

Jeanne: So tell me some more. You said they made it fun, tell me more, in as much detail as you can what you really liked about them.

Isabel: Um [pause], I'm not quite sure how to explain it. Like if I didn't understand something, Mr. B., for instance, we did almost like a Jeopardy type game and stuff like that for social studies, and he wouldn't be, how do I want to put it? —[he wasn't] serious-serious, like *mean* serious, if we got something wrong. He would help us explain what we got wrong, and then sometimes he would joke around about it, like "Oh well you were supposed get this right!" I don't know, he was more of the joking funny type teacher.

Jeanne: It sounds like two things. It sounds like, um, that he wasn't just trying to find out what you didn't know, but he was also then try-ing to *help* you [yes!] know what you needed to know.

Isabel: Yep, and he did it in more of a fun way, than just "Oh well, that's not right, it's da da da da da . . . "

Jeanne: Okay. So then the other thing I'm hearing is that you didn't come away feeling dumb or humiliated by how he would respond [right!] if you got something wrong [yes], like getting something wrong was okay.

Isabel: Yep, [laughs], that's both how Mr. B. and Mr. T. were.

Jeanne: Okay, any other things you can tell me about them that you liked?

Isabel: Not really, just pretty much that they helped explain things, and if I needed help they were there to help me with that subject.

Jeanne: And so you also felt very comfortable [yes] going to them.

Isabel: Yep.

When I make Isabel "queen for a day" and give her "unlimited power" to make changes at Comprehensive High, she says, "I would try to get some of the other teachers to be more like Mr. T. and Mr. B. Maybe set them down with them and have them tell them or show them how they taught me." I say, "You'd want other teachers to be able to develop the same kinda skill that Mr. B. had [yes] in allowing students to be wrong and then build-ing students' understanding on that?" "Yep," she answers, "and building their *confidence.*"

The second reason Isabel gives for dropping out was "the students themselves." "Which students?" I ask, and she identifies two groups at opposite ends of the peer hierarchy. The first group is the elite: the preps and jocks. Of this group, she says, "A lot of the so-called preps, the football players, the cheerleaders, they always thought they were better than others." *Inside* the classroom, these students shined, and served as a constant reminder to Isabel that she did not, especially in those classrooms where mistakes were unwelcome. *Outside* the classroom, these students were gatekeepers to the extracurricular activities Isabel wanted to participate in:

> There was a lot of stuff [at Comprehensive High] I wanted to do, but it was mostly the students that held me back from going and doing 'em. Like cheerleading, I used to cheerlead in elementary school and *loved* it. Sometimes I even wanted to play football [laughs], but the closest I got to the field was cheerleading, 'cause my dad wouldn't let me play football. But there was [pause], I felt that it was mostly for the preppy blonds and the girls that are always toothpicks, and stuff like that, and I'm not, I wasn't that big, but I wasn't the toothpick kind of person, so.

Extracurricular activities are, from the perspective of students active in them, often the most engaging and joy-filled part of the school day, so it's not surprising that relationships between participation in extracurricular activities and school persistence have been identified by a number of scholars (Christenson et al., 2001; Finn, 1989). Increasingly such participation is linked to social class resources. Athletes are expected to attend private training camps in the summer, participate in travel leagues outside of school, and often purchase their own uniforms and equipment. Budding musicians no longer have access to school instruments, but must purchase or rent them if they wish to join orchestra or band. Moreover, those with economic capital benefit from private lessons. Not only are such students likely to improve their talents through their private camps and lessons, they also have shared experiences that support the formation of friendships, the consolidation of elite status, and the active exclusion of young people like Isabel who do not have access to such resources.

The second group of students who haunted Isabel was located at the other end of the peer hierarchy. She describes them as kids who partied and did drugs, and who looked for weak students to target. Describing these bullies (Hodgson, 2008; Noguera, 2001), she says,

> There's a lot of students that, how do I wanna put it, got into a lot of fights and just started picking on people for no reason, and stuff like that, and

I was pretty much the person that got picked on all the time. And got followed home and stuff like that.

When I asked her why she thought she was a target, she says simply, "Because I wasn't like them." She didn't party, and more importantly, she wasn't *mean*. She just didn't have the disposition and demeanor required to fend off attacks. She did try to get help from teachers and administrators, and, as is often the case, this only made matters worse:

I went to the principal's office and told teachers about it, but they said they really couldn't do anything because they didn't actually catch them doing anything that harmful. And I kept telling 'em that and they said they'd watch out to make sure they wouldn't do anything and then because I did that, a lot of them started waiting till I got outside of school.

Isabel felt extremely isolated and vulnerable in school. Feeling like an outsider with both teachers and peers, she spent her days in a state of hypervigilance, and describes school as analogous to

Babysitting, 'cause you gotta pretty much babysit who's around you, make sure they're not—how do I put it?—[Babysitting is] pretty much the only thing I can think of that it's almost like, 'cause it's all kids, and you got the ones that think they're all that, and the immature ones, and stuff like that and *you gotta always watch your back*, and watch and make sure they're not doing something to harm somebody else or harm you.

Again, as queen for a day, Isabel says , "I'd probably make the people that picked on me all the time feel what it was like to get picked on, and go through the things that me and other people like me went through." But on reflection, she says, "I wouldn't be able to, 'cause I don't like being like other people, like thinking like that. I just don't like being the kind of person that's always mean to people."

For Isabel, high school was stressful *every single day*. Inside the classroom she experienced the extremes of humiliation and invisibility. Outside the classroom, she lived in fear. Moreover, the pain and frustration required to persist were not met with any tangible rewards. She was not making progress academically, she felt invisible to her teachers, and she was constantly the victim of peer abuse. At the time she made it, her decision to leave made real sense:

I didn't like going, and not only did I not get the help I needed, but I have people constantly nagging or whispering, like if you're in class or whatever, whispering and saying stuff about you or throwing papers or like trying to fight you outside or inside of school all the time. [I quit school] pretty much 'cause I felt all my grades were dropping and a lot of problems with the students, and I didn't feel like I was getting the help, so I didn't wanna stay in a place where I was supposed to get an education if I'm not getting it.

Isabel's sense that she is not to blame for her departure, however, is partial and muted by a common denial of her school wounds. Olson (2009) describes denial of school wounding as "one of our most popular educational discourses" and writes, "In the culture of school, where authority is rarely seated in the student, pupils often are encouraged to suck it up, to conform, to keep a stiff upper lip, and to understand that 'learning is hard, so deal with it'" (p. 85). One consequence of this is that students blame themselves: "If I had worked harder, been smarter, been more self-disciplined, I wouldn't have had those negative experiences in school" (Olson, 2009, p. 86). Isabel expresses this denial:

Up until now, pretty much, I think every day, I shoulda just stayed in school, 'cause I'm not getting the job that I wanna get and well it's harder to get a job that I wanna get, and stuff like that, and make a living without having an education, some kind of education. I wish I had the education I *need.*

In the structure of our contemporary school system, Isabel's lack of normative academic capital frames her as marginal and weak by her teachers. In the peer structure that accompanies this system, she lacks also the economic capital that facilitates elite membership, and is therefore framed a loser by those on top. In this same peer structure, other students likewise framed as losers frame Isabel as a target. In *The Challenge to Care in Schools,* Nel Noddings (2005) argues that the narrow academic goals of contemporary schooling, and the attendant "creation of rivals and enemies" (p. 54), should be replaced by a richer, humanist set of goals: "happy, healthy children; cooperative and considerate behavior; competence in the ordinary affairs of life; intellectual curiosity; openness and willingness to share; a confessed interest in existential questions and a growing capacity to contribute to and thrive in intimate relationships" (Noddings, 2005, p. 109). Isabel already possesses several of these qualities, qualities she has stubbornly maintained in the face of many assaults on them. How would Isabel be framed in Noddings' school?

7

Iris

A Voice not Heard

Schools [need to] listen to the kids; not just certain kids, but *all* the kids, 'cause that was one of my biggest problems—going, trying to get help, and *not being heard.* They need to listen to those kids. That's what they're there for, and they don't do their job, so how do they expect kids to do their job? Most kids that leave have similar problems that I do, though I have met a few that just drop out because they don't wanna attend anymore. I think that's ridiculous! But for the most part, kids who drop out, who want their education, aren't getting it. There's a *reason* why they're dropping out.

—Iris

It's one of those rare warm, sunny days in March. Iris sits waiting on her front stoop when I arrive to fetch her and take her back to my house for the interview. She's wearing faded blue jeans, a tee-shirt, a hoodie, and a dark teal knit beret. She has small gauges in each ear, and her eyes— "a deep moody chestnut, with splashes of yellow and dark green"[1]—peer out from under artfully contoured brows. The first of most of these interviews has taken place at the Youth Center, because for several of the

---

Canaries Reflect on the Mine, pages 61–68

young people who've spoken with me, the Center is a place where they feel supported; it's comfortable there. Iris, however, has asked *not* to be interviewed at the Center, and as we talk, I discover that there are few places and even fewer peers with whom Iris feels truly at home. In what appears *at first* as irony, Iris's self-imposed isolation stands in sharp contrast to her extraordinarily keen understanding of the value of social relationships. "I keep pretty much to myself," she tells me, over and again. Paradoxically, from a distant perch, Iris lays to waste the myth of the rugged individual. She is a rare gift to the sociologist; a wonderful anomaly who sees context and interaction wherever her gaze falls, and can tell her story with uncommon clarity and heartbreak.

Alongside Iris's sociological gifts sit her artistry, an artistry both natural and inspired by experience. This comes through even in the cadence of her voice. Listening to her interview again, I remember that she had a cold, and that I plied her with orange juice. You can hear how stuffed her nose is on the recording. And this encounter with her voice—made new by space, time, and reflection—produces such a longing to sit in conversation with her again, because in spite of the congestion and frequent sniffles, her voice has such a musical quality. Her frequent laughter—sardonic one moment, joyful the next—chimes. A simple sentence—imbued with subtle inflections and pensive pauses—conveys so much more than the string of words on a page.

Iris attended elementary school in the Comprehensive District, and then middle and early high school in another state, where she dropped out in ninth grade. Upon returning to upstate New York, she enrolled at Comprehensive High. It was a brief revisiting: "I only went for about half a year, before I couldn't take it anymore. I gave it another try, but it just wasn't working for me." On the face of it, Iris's experiences are most like Isabel's. Both young women identify the same two factors, in the same order of importance, in their decision to exit school: being neglected by teachers and being targets of peers. But her analysis of these experiences is most like Ivan's. Themes that are common to many of these stories—favoritism, unresponsive pedagogy, peer conflict—are spoken about less as individual troubles and more as social issues (Mills, 1959). Larger implications are acknowledged and named.

The perception of favoritism comes up first when I ask whether she was involved in any school activities. Iris says, "I was in art club, [but] I didn't get to *do anything*, and that was a big issue. I was pretty upset about that."

"When was that," I ask, "and what happened?"

"Sixth grade." She says,

Sixth graders got to be in art club, and [we] were going to paint the hall-ways. Well, a lot of the more popular kids were picked and those that really wanted to be involved weren't. That's a problem. Teachers will do that, pick certain groups of students and favor 'em, while the rest they don't interact with at all. And that's a problem I had [in my other school too]. [One] teacher separated her least favorite kids, and I was one of them, and we were the "problem" kids in her class. [In that school] the whole administra-tion, and everything, actually favored a lot of the more popular kids, those jocks and stuff.

Underneath the specific examples of favoritism is a deeper critique of the unequal valuing of different students, the unequal responsiveness to different ways of learning, and the unequal commitment to everyone's success. Like Adel, David, and Isabel, traditional pedagogy—listening to lectures, reading, taking notes, paper and pencil tasks—does not work for Iris. Describing, for instance, her challenges completing homework, she says, "Textbooks are a little confusing for me, 'cause I'm reading from one paper to the next, trying to find a quote from that reading [to put] into that, to find [my] answer, and sometimes it wouldn't make sense." Also like Adel, Iris believes that too many teachers value more highly those students who respond positively to traditional pedagogy, students who are, in effect, low maintenance receptors for the one directional transmission of estab-lished curriculum.

This is especially evident in Iris's experience with her most difficult sub-ject—math: "Math—I need help! I *permanently* need help from someone to teach it to me. I *can't* learn it on my own." Iris was placed in an Academic Intervention Service (AIS) lab for math, and assigned to the same teacher for her regular math class. She was lost in both, and begins to tell this story in response to my question, "What did you most dislike about Comprehen-sive High?"

She says, "I didn't like my counselor at all, and a teacher that I had, 'cause when I actually asked for help, I wasn't getting it, and I was *not liking that at all.*"

"So," I ask, "do you mean help with particular classes?"

The inflection of her simple "yeah," translates to, "Can you *believe* that?" This is the first time Iris asserts her *right* to support.

The story continues, and it is one of dogged persistence on her part, and her perception of indifference and disdain on the part of those with the power to help her. "I went up to [my math teacher] quite a few times. My first couple of days, I *flat out* told her I wasn't getting it—'I *need help* on this.'" The teacher's first response was to call Iris out, in front of the rest of the class, about her AIS placement: "Oh, you have *another* class with me [subtext: "You're an AIS student"], *maybe* you'll get it then" [subtext: "I don't have to deal with you here"]. From Iris's perspective, she was being told that the regular math class was for her teacher's *real* students, her *smart* students, and that the lab was for *losers* like Iris.

Despite this "nerve-wracking humiliation," Iris continued to ask for help. In addition, Iris's older sister—a very smart and tenacious woman— entered the fray, and began advocating for Iris with the teacher. In spite of Iris's own efforts and her sister's advocacy, the teacher continued to ignore Iris's repeated requests for assistance, and to simultaneously frame her as the problem. So, for instance, when Iris told her that the class notes were not enough to help her do her homework, she says, "[The teacher] made it sound like I had no intelligence *whatsoever*, and I just needed to learn how to *write* notes." Iris knows better:

> There's other ways around questions, and some teachers will show you a couple ways, while one teacher will show you one, and some teachers will just write notes and say, "Now do it." You can't just by notes. Each student learns differently. I know I'll learn something different from another student, like math. I'll learn it if someone sat down there, taught me how to do it, and if that'll *process* to me, but when you're just trying to teach everyone at once, and don't help kids individually, not all those kids are gonna get it.

Concluding that she had reached a dead end with her teacher, Iris next went to her guidance counselor, "to see if I could get a different teacher, *to help me learn*," she says. "And I was *rejected*," she adds.

"And what explanation did they give you?" I ask.

"There was no real explanation. The counselor made it seem like I was only trying to get in the class to be with certain people, and that wasn't my reason *at all*."

Rather than accommodating Iris's request for a different math teacher, her counselor recommended that she transfer to an alternative high school.

On his recommendation, Iris did visit the school, but she did not like it. She did not want to move to yet another school; she just wanted a different teacher for math. A quite reasonable request, one might argue, given the circumstances. At this point in the story, Iris expresses her sense—and her anger—that her guidance counselor is interested only in keeping her in school, not in supporting her learning: "I told him I didn't like the alternative school, and he was all disappointed about it. He was trying, like he tried *so hard* to *keep* me in school, but he wasn't helping me to *succeed* in school."

This lack of responsiveness to her needs as a learner converges with the second most powerful factor propelling Iris out of school: the poisonous social atmosphere at school and feeling unsafe. Like Isabel, she is a target. Isabel describes a state of hyper-vigilance—a need to constantly watch her back. Similarly, Iris says that relationships with peers are "nerve-wracking," and speaks of a pervasive sense of anxiety, especially during lunch, when anything can and too often does happen. At first, Iris pushes back: "I didn't really like this girl at all. All she did was run her mouth, and I *flat out* told her to *shut it.*" The girl responded by "getting this [other] girl *twice my size* to threaten me *right at lunch*" [blatantly out in the open]. Probing further, it becomes clear that Iris sees the negative traits of her peers—"stuck up," "rude," "vicious"—as less individual in nature, and more social. When asked for a metaphor for school, Iris steps back and assumes the stance of a sociologist. The consequences of meanness are seen in relation to the perpetrator as well as the victim. The context is bigger, the meaning more existential. Iris describes school this way:

> It's a drama fest. Everyone just pretty much hitting upon everyone, just *always* having to have problems with someone. Not only is that stressful for the person you're attacking, but if you look at it, you're making it much more harder on yourself, if you're going to attack someone. Life is more, more *complicated* than that, and everyone just, like everyone looks at it like it's just themselves, and you *can't live like that, you get nowhere.* I'm a teenager, but to me, I see people *differently* than I notice a lot of kids. I'm not the only one who sees the way I do, but there are a lot of kids out there who just don't use that common sense and respect. Respect is a *big* thing, I'll respect you if you respect me.

The indifference Iris experienced in academic matters is echoed, just as it was for Isabel, in the indifference of school staff to this drama fest. And just as Iris exposes the irony of attempts to *keep* her in school without helping her to *succeed* in school, she sees the actions of school staff with regard to bullying and peer conflict as empty lip-service to a problem no one wishes to examine too closely or to address in a substantive way.

> You're putting a bunch of kids together, the way they are. Then schools don't pay attention to what's *really* going on. They want you to go, be active and go *tell someone* about what's happening, and then when you do, they ignore the problem, until something bad happens. [Teachers and administrators] always *talk* about bullying and how bad it is, but they don't *do* anything about it. They make it out to be such a bad thing, but, like I said, they won't do anything about it.

Looking out through Iris's deep moody chestnut eyes, she sees herself in school, ostensibly to learn, but she's not learning. Not only is she not learning; she doesn't feel safe. What *can* she do? Well, first she stops going to her math class, the one that she tried so hard to get out of. And then, once she's left school to avoid math, it gets harder and harder to come back even for those classes she does like, such as biology, because coming back means returning to that poisonous, unsafe environment. And the one person she considers her friend, who she describes as having "similar problems," doesn't want to be in school any more than Iris does. Skipping school becomes an exercise of collective agency:

> I knew this girl, so for the most part I just sat with her every lunch period, and she had troubles in school too, so when she'd always be like, "I don't wanna be here!"—I didn't either, so we'd always leave.

I worry less about Iris than I do about Isabel for the simple reason that Iris sees quite clearly the relational nature of learning. She frames her ability to take responsibility for her part within the context of her teachers, her guidance counselor, and her administrators assuming responsibility for theirs. Isabel *wishes* her teachers had helped her more, but she does not feel *entitled* to such help. She knows she was doing her best, but still compares herself to the norm we have constructed for students, and finds herself coming up short. If she were a smarter student, a better student, if she had only stuck it out.... Iris, on the other hand, rejects the norm *flat out* (as she would say), and connects each of her failings to the failure of school personnel to do their jobs:

> Part of [dropping out] was my fault. Not going to classes, I can't just blame the school for that, but they kind of made me choose [to leave]. They wanted me to do something about it and my reaction was, well, if you're not gonna help me, I don't wanna help you. Like [the relationship between] not *understanding* homework and not *doing* homework. I never got it done, but I also was never understanding it.

Iris does not simply *wish* she had gotten more, she *refuses to settle* for less. "I didn't *wanna* drop out," she says, and adds, "I'd go back, *if* it was *different.*" And, like most of the young people who have talked with me, Iris is painfully aware of the social stigma and limited opportunities that have accompanied her decision. Asked what she thinks has been the worst consequence of dropping out, she says,

> *Criticism* [no hesitation]. I hate it. You'll still always get the drama. The drama is less, *especially when you keep to yourself,* but there are people out

there who you'll meet, and I've had a lot of criticism—"Oh, you're not smart enough 'cause you dropped out." Blah, blah, blah. That's not true in most cases, like in any case, really. Just 'cause you dropped out doesn't mean you're not smart enough. I don't like that, 'cause *I'm not stupid, I'm very intelligent.* Obviously I've gotten this far *on my own.* If I'm that stupid, then why am I still standing?

The other [worst] thing is trying to find a job is *so difficult.* You need a job to survive and I've been looking for a job for almost two years, and just no one really hires around here in the first place, but education does play a big part on it. And you could say I didn't graduate, and it seems like they don't want me, ah, but I'm sure if they talked to me and what not, they'd understand [that] I'm trying different ways to get my education. It's just like they don't care. Education matters. But at the same time, obviously I wasn't learning it *in* the school.

Iris's analysis of her difficulty finding a job echoes the contradiction she raised earlier about the fundamental difference between doing seat time in school and actually learning. Similar to her guidance counselor, who was more concerned about her attendance than her learning, prospective employers are more concerned about a credential than what she actually knows or can do. Iris has learned more and has learned better as a result of removing herself from a toxic school environment, but an employer would rather hire someone with a credential, no matter how hollow it may be.

In *The Sociological Imagination,* C. Wright Mills (1959) observes that without a sense of the larger world and their place in it, individuals are trapped in their *private orbits.* Within individuals' up-close and personal contexts, he suggests, they experience some degree of agency. But outside the confines of home, school, and work, they're overwhelmed by larger *impersonal* forces beyond their immediate control. Consequently, they find shelter in and cling to their private orbits and live as *vicarious spectators* outside of them (Mills, 1959, p. 3). Students who conform to the narrow role our society has ascribed for them experience the private orbit of the classroom as a space of agency, limited though it is. But the well-being they experience here comes at a cost to their agency beyond it. Iris, Ivan, and other young people with sociological sensibilities experience the reverse. The private orbit produces not well-being, but a more profound sense of entrapment, precisely because those who share it cannot see beyond it. Iris and Ivan cannot live in this small space, but can explore the world by sticking their thumbs out on the highway. At the time of this writing, Iris has hitchhiked from the east coast to the west coast and back again, three times. One kind of common sense interprets this as youthful naivety at best and all-out stupidity at worst. However, in a society that systematically denies young people independence and agency, another kind of common sense recognizes the value and affirms the courage of learning *of* the world by being *in* the world (Freire, 1970).

Iris's story, as she tells it, is a moving deconstruction of one flawed cultural myth after another: that all people learn the same way in the same time; that it's okay to choose students' teachers for them and to force them to remain with teachers who do not support their learning; that the curriculum is more important than the learner; that the completion of 22 Carnegie Units of coursework means you've learned something of value; that peer meanness and victimization are inevitable developmental stages, rather than socially constructed phenomena. How many eighteen year olds do you know who possess this depth of insight into the human condition? Iris is right. She is *very intelligent* indeed.

Reflecting on Iris's keen sociological analysis of her school experiences and her decision to withdraw, I mourn for her and for what she has been denied, but I mourn also for what her peers and teachers have lost as a result of her departure from school. Schools and classrooms desperately need students who possess Iris's insights and moral sensibilities, her wisdom and grace. Students who can, in the words of Maxine Greene (1988), "surpass the given and look at things as if they could be otherwise" (p. 3). What might our schools and classrooms be like if we were willing to *hear* Iris, and others like her?

8

Ivan

Loss of Faith

seasonal headwear—by Ivan

It was spirit week at the high school and the only week where you can wear hats.

I was particularly fond of this week, though it having nothing to do with school spirit.

It was just a nice chance to break the mold and look ridiculous for five days a year.

It was first period with Mr. Duright's class, on Hat Day. I was wearing my dark blue bandanna tied over my long blond hair, which complemented my shirt quite well.

Mr. Duright, entered the room. Ominously.

Mr. Ivan take it off.

. . . excuse me Mr. Duright?

You heard what I said, Mr. Ivan. Take it off.

I looked around the room. It *was* in fact Hat Day. Directly behind me was a girl wearing one of those oversized, neon green foam cowboy hats, completely blocking the view of the person behind her. But nonetheless—

Mr. Ivan, take it off.

But why, Mr. Duright?

I knew why. A blue bandanna could represent gang activity—a gang which I certainly was not in.

But Mr. Duright decided to take a different approach—

It's not seasonal headwear.

Seasonal headwear!

I looked around the room. It was January, and not a single person was wearing a winter hat.

Mr. Ivan, take it off.

This was war! I was completely insulted. I was not a Crip. I was a fucking hippie. This was completely embarrassing, me being the only person forced to take his or her hat off on Hat Day.

The next day I wore my bright plaid flannel lounge pants to school. Which were also against the rules, even on spirit week (after the great pajama epidemic), except for pajama day, which this day certainly was not.

Mr. Ivan, take them off.

Whatever do you mean Mr. Duright?

Those pants are against school code and you need to take them off. If you have nothing else to wear I suggest you go to the main office and ask for a pair of pants from the lost and found. Regardless, take them off.

Embarrassed, I sulked my way to the front of the class and out the door. Everything was Ok though, I had a pair of gym shorts in my bag.

My pair of bright red skin tight basketball shorts from what must have been the 1970's that hung down quite literally no further than my dick. Which in fact, on most occasions, hung down farther than these shorts did. It all depended on the way I was standing really. They actually complemented my button up pastel collared shirt quite well though. Hmm. Should I tuck it in? No . . . too much.

I liked the way that if I left my shirt untucked it looked as if I were wearing nothing at all down there. My pale chicken legs glowing blindingly under the bright fluorescent light.

I walked back into the classroom. No, I *sauntered* back into the classroom. Everybody saw. There was nothing in the school dress code against boys' athletic shorts. In fact, many kids from lower income families—that's all they ever wore to school. Although considerably longer than mine I must say.

Mr. Duright looked up from his work. He examined me from top to bottom. I looked like some woman who had just had sex and was wearing the dude's shirt around the house. My long hair didn't help.

Thank you, Mr. Ivan.

He was apparently pleased, or at least satisfied, with my wardrobe adjustment.

This was all too much for the class, who at most times were too nervous to say or do anything around him. Some kids just smirked.

I sat down in my chair and mused over the fact that my lounge pants were against school code but these ridiculous shorts were quite alright, though they were in no way seasonal legwear. Either way, it was declared a victory in the end. But this was all hearsay. It was all in my head anyways. Everything was in those days.

Score: Mr. Duright—1, Ivan—1

I've known Ivan for most of his life. He and my son, Nick, attended the same elementary school, were assigned to the same junior high teams, and shared many teachers and classroom experiences over the years. When they were 13, Ivan talked Nick into attending the National Guitar Workshop, and for the next three years they roomed together for a week each summer, immersing themselves in music and in the culture of musicians. In high school, they played together in a band featuring original music and instrumental versatility. Switching instruments between songs was a signature of their performances.

From the sidelines, I'd been watching Ivan grow up for years, and when Nick came home one day during their junior year and announced, "Ivan dropped out," I was *stunned*. Almost immediately my shock turned to skepticism. Nick had been lobbying hard to drop out himself. Was this *another* ploy? So I called Ivan's mom, and she confirmed the news—somewhat apologetically, I might add, because she knew Nick was hanging on by a thread.

All of the young people I've talked with defy the hollow stereotypes we attach to dropouts. Ivan is no exception. Selected for the district's talented and gifted program in elementary school, and honors and accelerated classes in junior and senior high school, Ivan was an outstanding student academically. He was also involved in school sponsored athletics, music, and theater. In his own words,

> As a young kid, my grades were *perfect*. I mean I hate to brag, but I was a *fucking awesome student*. I was a *great* student. I was the *teacher's pet*. I did everything. I went above and beyond, clubs and this and that. And it was fun, and it was okay when I was able to do that because I believed fully in the school system and what it could do for you.

At the heart of Ivan's decision to leave school was what he refers to as a "loss of faith" in the value of schooling:

> There came a point in time where I just stopped believing in high school. I started to question whether the high school experience was worth the outcome, worth the results that high school gives you. Because it lasts so long, on and on into college. And when I really evaluated what was important to me in life, I decided that high school was more of a side project, something to get over with so that I could have the degree, when really I was just studying the things important to me on the side, separate from high school. So high school just kinda got in the way.

Losing faith was not an overnight process. It began in tenth grade when Ivan became keenly aware of the mental and physical constraints imposed by the school system. In a long narrative, Ivan chronicles this period:

> There came a time in tenth grade, when I really started to just question everything. I did not feel good. I felt depressed. I felt very overloaded, and I felt really rebellious. I felt part of a system that was geared toward chugging out these *normal* kids and it wasn't personalized. In tenth grade, they would put work in front of me, they would put classes in front of me, and I would go, "Why?" I mean every kid does that. "Why we gotta do this, why we gotta do that?" You know? [Long pause] Let's just say in tenth grade, I was very unhappy, and school was not making me any happier. I was not enjoying being in school, I was not enjoying doing the homework they had me doing, I was not getting along with some of the teachers, I was not getting along with any of the students. I felt trapped in this place, this *very unwelcoming place*, that just demanded so much of me, that I couldn't understand the worth. "Why?" That's all I kept saying. "Why? Why do this? Why do this?"
>
> I would sit there, and I would look at the day outside—a bright, sunny, beautiful day—and I would just ask myself, "What's going on out there?" I mean, "I'm here. Why am I here? There's no one chaining me to here, but yet here I am." And I felt like I was just *slaving* over everything and I didn't have enough mental capacity to keep chewing on what they were feeding me, you know? It's as if they would put a paper in front of me, and I'd just write a big

fucking *why*? on it. Why do you want me to do this? What's it worth? What's the use? Where is this going?

Then I made it through tenth grade, but my grades started to drop, and part of this had to do a lot with my health. I had just sustained a neck injury that made it very uncomfortable for me to sit still for long periods of time, and my neck was always sore, and I had trouble sleeping. I was very tired. I was very irritable. I was very in pain. And I was very nervous too. I had anxiety issues. I think that some of it had to do with smoking weed. I did that back in the day,[1] and I started having just these weird panic attacks, that I think spawned from using marijuana. But I also think that using marijuana actually was another cause of me just questioning everything, you know? I started to reevaluate my whole world, my whole existence, and I remember that my downfall in school was this essay I had to write.

We were in English class and I didn't get along with the English teacher, and she said, "Okay, you know what, here's a *fun* one for you guys. We're going to write essays on a question. You can pick any question you want. Just answer a question with an essay." And I was sitting there and I thought—I was the fucking class clown—and I thought it'd be funny: Okay—"What is the meaning of life?" Ha, ha! And that was my question, and she thought it was stupid and I *knew* it was stupid, but you know I was just being a joker.

But then I thought, why not pursue this? Why not pursue this question? It's always the *big* question for everyone, so I decided I would just check out some of the major religions and find their take on what the meaning of life is, right? So I did this kinda study of all the major religions of the world. But this essay was what really sparked this weird transformation, this weird philosophical transformation in my mind, which ended up ultimately causing this crazy disinterest, and this crazy rebellion against school. Because eventually, when I wrote my essay, [what] came out from all of it, is that it is a *miracle* to be alive, it is a *beautiful thing* to be alive, to be living your life, your freedoms, your spirituality, your love, your passions, the things that interest you. It's a miracle! Every moment on this earth is a miracle, and it's wonderful. And I just kept asking myself the question during all this, "Then why am I filling my life, *these prime years of my boyhood* and my physical prime with this *slavery*, this mental, this physical slavery, sitting here in this ugly child factory?" You know? Why am I writing this essay? And I just kinda stopped from that point on. I stopped doing my homework, because from that point on, every moment outside of school was what I just really became interested in.

Then comes the summer, okay? And the summer was *brilliant*. I did so many things that summer. I slept in a tent more than I did a building that summer. I went on two-week backpacking trips, festivals, music, brilliant things, you know, in this summer after tenth grade. And suddenly I'm flung right back into school in eleventh grade, and all of a sudden the pain in my neck came back. I was sleeping less than three hours a night during eleventh grade—the year I dropped out of school. I would go to school. I would sit there. It was all just a joke to me eventually. I wasn't doing my homework. I would sit there in school and laugh at just the ridiculum of all of these things they were telling me. Everything was just so funny to me, and I was getting worn out. I was not sleeping. I was not doing homework. I'd go home and that would suddenly be my big opportunity to fill my life with meaningful things, and I would be up late into the night, just doing the things that I wished I could of accomplished. And I was learning things. I was studying Buddhism, I was studying all these Eastern philosophies and what not. I was missing days of school, and they're saying my grades were bad, and my attendance was bad, right? And *everything was just bad*, you know. And I was going crazy. But I'm still chugging at it though, 'cause high school's high school. What're you gonna do? You gonna drop out? *Only fucking losers drop out of high school*, you know what I mean? I'm fucking, you know, I'm an honor roll kid here, what's going on?

But eventually, it just got too bad, and I started having emotional breakdowns and mental breakdowns and anxiety breakdowns and everything. It just all came to a head, half way through eleventh grade, and what made it easiest eventually to finally drop out of school was that it became apparent that the school was *not on my side*. The school viewed me as some screw up, some nasty, spoiled something, ah, what's the word? Manipulative kid! Right? This *monster* that didn't belong there anymore, I guess. It became apparent that *the school was against me*, it was working against me, and at that point in time, I said, "Well, if you don't want me here, I don't want to be here!" and, ah, I never went back. And at the head of this army—it didn't even seem like it was me versus the school, it seemed like it was me versus [a principal] and [a teacher]. I mean, the principal acted like his school was his castle. This was his domain, and if he wasn't on your side then you weren't having it. He was definitely against me, and at this point in time I felt like school was the enemy, and they felt like I was the enemy, and we split in a not-so-good feeling way.

In the period leading up to this split, Ivan went from a compliant, straight-A student to a daily resister, refusing to remain silent in classes where his questions were unwelcome, refusing to stay "in place" when his neck screamed for movement or his passions called him elsewhere. Ivan's increasingly frequent refusals to submit to the constraints of schooling led to multiple disciplinary referrals—"Referrals for sleeping in class, referrals for leaving class, referrals for doing other things than your mandated schedule." Each referral escalated the antagonism between Ivan and his principal, giving way eventually to the administration's refusal to make any accommodations for Ivan's neck injury.

Because Ivan had always been such a strong student, he had entered his junior year with considerable surplus credits. His mother, armed with medical documentation, requested a health related Individual Education Plan (IEP) to reduce Ivan's total hours of seat time and allow him to begin later in the day, so that he could get more sleep. She was initially stunned by the brick wall she hit, a point she has confirmed in multiple conversations with me. Ivan describes both the brick wall and his mother coming around to viewing the situation as he did:

> Oh it was a power struggle [between the principal and me]. And as you can see, that struggle there, my mother did not understand. [The struggle is] the reason I received no sympathy [for my neck injury]. [Laughs]. 'Cause they saw a bright young man who was *ruining everything.* [Laughs]. And then all of the sudden for my mom to go, "His neck injury, it hurts him, he's not sleeping, and he's slowly losing it," [when] I was still puttin' up the good fight as best as I could. They were like, "Yeah, well this kid's not getting any sympathy 'cause he's causing *so much trouble with everyone.*" So I realized there would be no sympathy given, and when my parents—or at least just my mom—saw that they had this attitude toward me, that made it okay for me to just leave, for me to drop out of the race, and that's how eventually I accomplished [dropping out].

Ivan's journey to the exit was complicated; there's a lot to tease out in this period of losing faith and growing resistance. One factor that he alludes to in passing was his relationship with peers—"I was not getting along with any of the students." Ivan offers a fuller context for this in another part of an interview:

> Honestly, I [pause], I was always trying to find my niche in high school, and I never did. I never really felt like I fit in with the sports crowd, and I never really fit in with the kind of academically charged crowd, and so I just kinda would float to whoever seemed like the most comfortable to be around at the time, you know. But with school insecurity, you know, sometimes you're unsure of where you belong in the whole scheme of things.

Eventually, Ivan says his "lack of ability to connect" made him feel as if he "didn't belong anywhere." This inability to connect emerges out of the intensely reflective frame of mind that Ivan is experiencing. The big "why?" question permeates nearly every experience and relationship he encounters. With peers Ivan finds no substance. He expresses this in his analysis of the stratification system at school:

> The whole social order, the pecking order, how kids section themselves off from one another, for me it's all money. I mean if you've got the money, some people don't even need the social skills, you know. You're just kinda flung up there with all the other kids with the money. They don't have to be good at school, they don't have to be good at anything, really. They're just kind of up there.

If Ivan could find little of value in relationships with most peers, he was growing even more skeptical of the value of school learning itself, which he experienced as overwhelming and oppressive on the one hand—"I felt like I was just slaving over everything and I didn't have enough mental capacity to keep chewing on what they were feeding me"—and irrelevant on the other:

> I say school is a system. It's a factory. It's a *child factory*. The children file in. They're in there, they're being *tinkered* with, and then they're bussed out. That really made me angry. It's a system. It's *rigid*, and you're put in one end, and you're *blown* out the other, and in the middle they *inject you with information, they're constantly injecting you*, into your head, information. It doesn't matter if you want to know it. *It doesn't matter if it matters.* It's just whatever the curriculum [dictates].

When I ask him who he thinks is responsible for this system, and what they hope to achieve, the following exchange ensues:

Ivan: Well I think it became apparent that "educated people" were what everyone wanted to be. I wanna be an educated person, and they're like, "Well, you know, we can create a public school system where everyone can be educated. We will teach everyone everything there is to know." Apparently. And what came out of that is they required subjects of English and math and history and stuff like that.

Jeanne: If it's a system, and they take you in and they shoot you out, what is it they want in the end when they shoot you out?

Ivan: Oh, just an educated population.

Jeanne: Okay, so you say you think they want to shoot out an educated person, but it doesn't sound like what you're talking about. I mean, it sounds like a really strange definition of educated.

Ivan: Well, it's *very thinly spread.* The education that they inflict upon you is spread thinly in all areas, you know. They make you take all areas, they make you take a language, you know all these different subjects, all these different electives, so you come out really knowing pretty much *a little* about *everything.* And my problem with the whole system is they go very in-depth about the things like math, and different areas of English. They pretty much want an educated population to come out so that we can all get good jobs and be smart citizens, but why? Why calculus? Why does every student in the public school system need to get all the way to pre-calculus and crazy statistics, circle proofs, crazy theories? It's required, and it pertains to *nothing* in this universe even that anyone would ever kind of get into unless you're in such careers as engineering or space travel. Yet, we are doing it for *months* at a time, you know. It seems like as long as they're keeping us there, they might as well just *drill* as much as they can into our heads. You know what I mean?

Jeanne: So I'm hearing, I'm hearing a few different things. One thing I'm hearing is what some researchers call a "mile wide and inch deep curriculum."

Ivan: Right!

Jeanne: But the other thing I'm hearing—

Ivan: [Interrupts] Is that it's not just an inch deep. I don't even think it's a mile wide and inch deep. I think it's a mile wide and very deep, [but] what you come out of high school with is not a mile wide and not even an inch deep, because you don't retain any of this information. You learn it so that you can remember it for the next week so that you can pass your test, and then once it's gone, I mean once you're done with it, it's gone, it flies away, you know? So what you're doing, really, is you're learning this information so that you can pass your test either at the end of the month or the end of the week or the end of the year, but as soon as you're done with that, you don't retain it. *You* come out an *inch deep*, but the education that runs through you—they get so into detail on everything thing—it's like they're trying to *cram* so much into you. So the public school system is actually a mile wide and very deep, *but the end result is nothing.*

Believing that the end result is nothing—"I don't put value on over 90% of it, honestly"—Ivan becomes less and less willing to exert the energy needed to perform at high levels.

This forms the back story for Ivan's observation—"I was not getting along with some of the teachers." As he becomes more conscious of the conflict between his own interests and desires and what he is required to focus on in school, different types of teachers become visible to him. First, there are the teachers who give him the information he needs to progress in school in already digestible form—ready to swallow, no chewing required. It is with these teachers he feels the greatest solace; with these teachers he doesn't "remember ever feeling trapped. It was never a struggle." Describing one such teacher, he says,

Every day, he would do the same sort of sort of outline of our topic. He would very clearly and concisely tell us what we need to know. We'd go over it. Each homework assignment was clearly and concisely put out there for us. Everything was very clear, concise, simple, you know. It was like an easy ride through. The information was served to you on a silver platter. You serve it back to him on a silver platter. He was very helpful, and the tests were very straightforward. Pretty much he was there to teach you this subject, and he was not there to make it *hard* for you, and you just rode through his class. I mean we learned it, we all learned what we were supposed to, and it wasn't hard, you know. *Why should it be so hard?*

Ivan's multiple descriptions of teachers and classes such as these seemed counterintuitive to me. After several probes, I finally said, "Ivan, okay when you say these teachers did not make it *hard*, I'm trying to wrap my mind around that, because in your case I've known you since you were really small. You're very bright, and you've never struck me as someone who was disinclined to be challenged." After an extensive back and forth, my synapses fired, and his perspective finally became clear to me. Within the context of being *forced* to learn about things that had no value to him, he was especially grateful to teachers who painlessly gave him what he needed, without expecting him to engage his finite energies in learning their subjects *outside* of class. He did not, in fact, desire engaging pedagogy and hands-on learning, if it meant more work for him on something for which he had no passion. In his words,

> I really enjoyed these teachers that, you know, when they had their forty minutes of class time, they just make it painless, quick and easy for you. So when I was trying my best to get through high school, to just get through it you know—I stopped concentrating on how well I was doing and how perfect everything needed to be, and just did the bare minimum—these classes that I was able to do the bare minimum and still keep that passing grade and not have problems with the teachers, you know those are the ones I really look back fondly on.

From Ivan's perspective, his teachers owned him for nearly seven hours each day. If they couldn't teach him what they needed to during those hours, then the problem was theirs, not his. His desire to be painlessly fed the mandated curriculum, *during school hours*, is made especially clear in reference to an AP course he ended up dropping. He says that his teacher would

> talk about things that didn't really pertain to what we were supposed to be doing in our curriculum. So during her class was time for her to kind of inflict her viewpoints upon us, or even just go off on tangents. That meant that we had to make up for all of our lost time at home doing these insane packets, from the ten pound fucking workbook, *for hours*, you know, as if her

class was just sit and relax time and then at home is where we learn [the subject], and that was not a good idea. I ran out of her class as soon as I could.

Of another teacher, Ivan says,

Some [of the homework] was memorizing vocabulary words that no one would ever use in their lifetime. And I just thought it was funny, because he once took me out of class, he took me aside, and we had this conversation. And he said, "Ivan, you seem to be two different students at the same time." I go, "I don't know what you're talking about." And he goes, "Well if we look here at your grade history," he says, "I look and I see 100, 74, 100, 59, 94, 79," and he goes, "What's going on here?" And I go, "Well, see, the 100s are when I actually bothered to take the time to look at your stupid vocabulary words that night, and the 74s are when I just didn't bother." [Laughs]. And he goes, "Oh, well, then I see that *you* see what you have to do now," or something like that. And I go, "Yeah, sure." [Laughs]. It became painfully obvious that if someone took the time to memorize these vocabulary words the previous night, then they could get 100s on these tests, and if they didn't then this is what happened.

If Ivan had a problem with teachers who "expect you to go above and beyond" and "want your 100%, 100% of the time, all day, every day," he had an even bigger problem with teachers who "want you to accept everything about them and their class, and if you don't really fit in and you don't really *agree*, there's going to be a power struggle." Power struggles such as these emerged with teachers who turned ambiguity into hard and fast rules, teachers who shut down students whose views diverged from their own. One such teacher became a lightning rod for Ivan's alienation:

Our relationship was really complicated because at first we really enjoyed each other. I sat at the front of his class with a big smile on my face every day. He would be throwing out jokes, me and him would be joking back and forth, and it was a lot of fun. But then as things kinda deteriorated, as my relationship with the school in its entirety deteriorated, and as my health and mental status deteriorated, so did mine and his relationship.

There were these pillars of the high school that I was eventually kind of at war against, that I was fighting against. And he was one of them. Because he represented this straight, hard, steadfast, rule-abiding thing that held a lot of power within the high school. I don't hold anything against him except for his complete disliking of me, his complete *disdain* for me, because that's the only thing that really caused conflict. Me and him eventually started clashing because when he would be throwing out all of these iron-clad theories and philosophies, I would question him. I think eventually he just didn't know what to do with that.

Like just as a small example, using proper English. You weren't allowed to say "yeah" in his class, you were only allowed to say "yes." So this was like a long running joke. You say "yeah," he'll go *"yes,"* and then you have to repeat yourself *"yes."* At first, I just thought this was hilarious, you know, the one period, 40 minutes per day, you can't say "yeah." So, instead of always repeating *"yes,"* I wrote down on my folder all the words that also meant "yes," like "affirmative!" and "indubitably!" and "Yes sir!" And he saw this. It was this little list taped on my folder labeled "yeah words."

Jeanne: And did he seem to appreciate this?

Ivan: Yeah, yeah, it was a joke between me and him. Indubitably! But what eventually happened was that just in terms of philosophical thinking, [his] position is that there is the proper way to speak English. You say "yes." You say the proper words. But with my way of thinking, the English language is a constant ever-morphing, changing, developing, um, it's fluid, it's changing. So maybe this old relic gets mad every time someone says "yeah," but we're adding new words into the dictionary every year of our lives, you know? Shakespeare added words that were not proper English, but he said 'em, he put them in popular culture and he made them words. Words in the dictionary! Now we have our slang, we have our African American slang, we have our Latino, like different things that come into the melting pot of America, that are not proper English now, that eventually will be. Such as "yeah." Everyone says "yeah." No one says "yes" anymore. So in a sense, his clinging on to the idea of proper English, I just thought was comical. You can believe what he was trying to impose on us, or you can realize that it's a lost cause.

Over time, and within the context of the overall deterioration Ivan refers to, he came to believe that this teacher was only open to "talk back" when it supported his purposes. He could joke with Ivan about the "yeah list" because the "yeah list" supported his aim of getting students to use proper English. What he could not do, however, was entertain a fundamental challenge to his world view about the English language itself. When Ivan moved from the "yeah list" to serious questions about the merits of the standard form and the future of the language, the teacher shut him down:

The argument that he always fell back on, when our exchange would actually kind of get really involved, he would then snap, "Oh this is wasting class time!" But in a sense, if you're going to stand up in front of your class and throw something out, and then not allow any conversation about it [Pause]. Fine, fine, I'm sorry I said something.

"Fine, fine, I'm sorry I said something," signifies Ivan's eventual retreat. Moreover, this retreat had to be total, not partial. He could not retreat *with-*

in the classroom; he had to retreat *from* it. It is, therefore, simultaneously an act of retreat and refusal. It is a refusal to participate in an education that substitutes a curriculum of the trivial for the passions and interests of the learner. It is a refusal to participate in an education that speaks loudly about things that matter little, while enforcing silence about questions of consequence.

Ivan's exit and its aftermath are infused with as much ambiguity and dissonance as the English language he fought so fiercely about. "Only fucking losers drop out of high school" is juxtaposed to a fundamental uncertainty about the very nature of winning and losing. This juxtaposition raises the question, "What do winners lose, and losers win?" This is the contradictory space Ivan occupies:

> I don't know if I'm your typical school dropout or not, but it just seems like with my story here, there's a mix of "I *wanted* to" [drop out] and then "I *had* to" [drop out]. That thing always goes back and forth in my mind. You know, yes, I didn't believe in school any more, but I would've never taken the large step of not going to school, I would never have jumped off that cliff until I had to. And I *had* to.
>
> I have a friend, Jim. He always talks about how the college he's in is such bullshit—"This is bullshit" and "Why am I doing this?" When his true passion is building houses. And he's ranted at me—'I just wish I could just get out of school and just start building houses!" And he's going to school to be some kind of chemistry teacher, or something like that. Everyone is too scared to take that step in that direction, 'cause it's *so scary*, you know? Look at our valedictorian, goes to [Ivy League University] now. From the time he was [pause], how old was he? He was 10. I've known that kid since he was 10. Every day after school, he would come up and say, "You know what's dumb? How we have to *keep* learning this?" And he'd sit there with his homework, with his pencil in his hand, and he'd be like, "And what is this? What is this? I mean, why we gotta do this?" You know, same old student complaining. Only this kid dotted every "i" and crossed every "t." He hated every ounce of homework that he had to do, yet he did it as perfect and he put as much time into it as he possibly could. Top of his class. [Ivy League] student. *Everyone* hates it, *everyone*. Everyone is unhappy with the school system in one way or another. But they go there for their friends, they go there because they're expected to, they go there because what else, what the fuck else are you gonna do?
>
> I just wish that there was some way to instill the bravery to kids that, that maybe there is something else out there. I mean, I've been out of the education loop for three years and I consider it my life. The times I was in school I feel like a little baby, you know, like someone who, who never made it out of the rooms. And then suddenly I was [out]. It's like the world was there. There's flowers, and there's beautiful things and there's all these crazy things. And

I always wondered what was out there when I was sitting in class, you know. And then I went and saw it. I went traveling, I went and did this and that and the other thing. And I'm just happy that even though I wasn't brave enough to do it, I *had* to do it. And I wish, and I think, that someday maybe other people will just become brave enough to not buy into a system like that, and go after their dreams. Like Jim and his house building, you know. He's not going to drop out of college, you know. He can't. There's too much expected of him. I mean everyone gets stuck in these jobs or in these situations where they just keep doing it, because what else are they going to do, you know, they're expected to do it, they're expected to stick at their jobs, they're expected to continue with their education.

[In school] years go by, you know weeks would go by like a second, and I don't remember what happened during that week. I don't remember. And the next week didn't look any better. It was just like "Wow! This is insanity! This is not how I want my life to be." I think it's been the greatest thing dropping out of high school, greatest thing in my life, you know. I don't know, I'm not gonna project it onto everyone else, but, you know, the three years that I haven't been involved in all that feel like two lifetimes.

How would you score this match? Who's the loser? The dropout or the valedictorian?

9

Canaries in the Mine

Honestly, I condemn the school system. I thought it was so much beyond repair that I've never given [reform] much thought, how I would change it. You know? I'm like, I'm done! I'm gonna think about me, and you know, as far as repairing the school system, I'm like, "Yeah, good luck!" I'll leave that to all the unfortunate people in it, you know, who are still in it. (Ivan)

I just hope school gets better 'cause I have a daughter on the way in. I really don't want—I've been almost afraid—to have her go to [Comprehensive Schools], 'cause of things I went through. I just hope there's a way that it can get better and the teachers and stuff can all be more helpful, maybe. (Isabel)

The juxtaposition of Ivan's deep-seated cynicism and Isabel's fragile hope speaks to the tension between the agency of students and teachers and the multitude of structural constraints under which they toil. Ivan's story and his larger critique of schooling—"It's a system, it's rigid!"—reflect a keenly intuitive understanding of structural constraints. Isabel's larger story is shaped as strongly by these constraints, but her joy-filled memories of teachers like Mr. B. speak also to the power of human agency, kindness, and care in schools.

I've spent nearly my whole life in public schools, and I've been a teacher, observer, and scholar of public education for over twenty-five years. When I began this project, I already possessed a big-picture understanding of the agency-structure tension in schooling. I was well versed in the competing philosophical aims and cultural contradictions that have shaped U.S. public schooling since Thomas Jefferson first proposed such a system in 1778. I had a sociologist's understanding of the stubborn workings of bureaucracies. I could juxtapose the language of standards, efficiency, competition, and accountability to the—in my view—far more compelling language of creativity, dialogue, collaboration, and growth that inspires teachers and students to work together with shared purpose. Each language expresses a different *common sense*, and I could identify the underlying assumptions about the purposes of schooling in both.

In spite of everything I knew, the many conversations I had with Hannah, Ivan, Steve, and the others revealed my own unexamined common sense. By seeing dropouts as somehow qualitatively "different" than young people who persist to graduation, I was looking for answers specific to them. What I've discovered instead is that what these young people experienced, and, more importantly, what these young people *wanted* from school are not unique to dropouts. Transcending their unique life stories, four themes emerged, themes that speak more generally to the needs and desires of all public school students, to all human beings, really.

Theme One: Being *Known*

> Each student learns differently, like I know I'll learn something different from another student. I'll learn it if someone sat down there, taught me how to do it, and if that'll *process* to me, but when you're just trying to teach everyone at once, and don't help kids individually, not all those kids are gonna get it. (Iris)

Iris's simple wisdom is shared by all good teachers. Every young person in this study had needs that were specific to them, and consistent with the participants in Carol Gallagher's (2002) study, each one felt that "their unique needs were not addressed by teachers or school officials" (p. 45). Brown and Rodriquez (2009) offer the concept "educational neglect" to signify the denial of learning support tailored to the diverse needs of individual students. Significantly, this neglect happens across the spectrum of academic performance. Isabel's experience with targeted academic intervention services is a case in point:

[Teachers] were supposed to sit there and help the individuals by themselves, and stuff like that, and pretty much I didn't feel they were doing that. They were helping all of us at one time, but they weren't helping specific people on specific things, like I needed.

From the perspective of the struggling student, this is a no-win situation. The "standards" are externally imposed, but the means of achieving them are denied. This irony is not lost on Iris:

The strongest things pushing me out? Teachers not teaching me! And like the fact that I was *trying* to get my education, but they didn't care about my education, they just cared about keeping me in school. And that felt unfair to me. Why should I stay in school if I'm not learning anything?

The message Iris felt that she was getting was that as long as she did not officially drop out, school personnel felt they were successful with her. Her critique is consistent with Dynarski and Gleason's (2002) review of federally funded, targeted drop out programs that found that alternative middle schools increased retention but had no measurable effect on student learning (see also Christenson et al., 2001), and supports Noddings' (2005) observation that, "[Students] suspect that we want their success for our own purposes, to advance our own records, and too often they are right" (p. 13).

Like Iris, Nathan attributed the lack of support for his learning to careless teachers: "[Teachers] just weren't there to help me for stuff I needed help with. *A lot of 'em didn't care,* and they didn't take the time to help out a lot of students, prob'ly 'cause there's so many people there." The reality is more complicated than a simple dichotomy of caring and careless teachers, or even classes that are too large to nurture intimacy and responsiveness. As Noddings (2005) has so compellingly argued, caring is not an individual attribute that some possess and others lack; it's a relationship between the carer and cared-for. Success depends on shared understanding and mutual engagement. The teacher must know the student fully enough to respond appropriately to her needs, and the student must perceive the care given as consistent with the needs she is experiencing. Noddings (2005) writes, "Most teachers work very hard and express deep concern for their students. In an important sense, teachers do care, but they are unable to make the connections that would complete caring relations with their students" (p. 2).

Making such connections requires a particular disposition on the part of teachers, one that recognizes the student as a whole person and considers the complexity of the student's life circumstances. It requires, in the words of William Ayers (2001), "kidwatching" (p. 136). But this is not enough. Completing the caring relationship requires a structure flexible enough to allow teachers to respond appropriately to the biographies and needs of their students. Our current structure, characterized by one-size-fits-all curricula and standardized measures of learning, disrupts relations of care.

Just as individual students come with various learning styles and different needs for *academic support*, so, too, their needs for *social support* vary. Some children and youth come to school well nurtured and cared for. Others, like Cole, Steve, and Hannah, come from circumstances that are, in the words of Ayers (2001), "out of balance, in need of repair" (p. 136). Schooling too often ignores or denies how this larger world "smothers and challenges and shapes and touches the child" (Ayers, 2001, p. 136). Hannah, a foster child involved in a destructive intimate relationship, needed someone to listen to what was going on in her life. In her words, her perfect teacher was someone who would say, "You have a problem? Okay, I'll help you." Struggling against the sharp edges of a mother's abandonment, Steve needed adults "that you could go and talk to, and they could help guide you. And maybe they could—if they had enough power—then maybe they could help you out."

Hannah and Steve needed more care of a certain kind. One common sense will say, "Well that's just not fair. Why should Hannah and Steve get more than someone else? It's only fair to treat everyone the same." But another common sense, expressed beautifully by Ayers (2001) in the passage below, understands the power of context. This common sense recognizes that to care more intensely for the child who needs it the most at any given time is to care better for all the children or youth in one's class:

> It is important for teachers to be fair, to be thoughtful, to be caring in relation to all students. If students were the same then a good teacher would treat them all the same. But here is Sonai with an explosive anger that can take over the room, and she needs more; here is James, whose mother died recently, and he needs more; here is Angel, who cannot speak English, and he needs more. Needs shift and change. . . . Helping the two children in kindergarten who are having difficulty separating from their mothers assures all children that this is a safe and friendly place. Good teachers spend time and energy where they must, and expect that positive results will spread laterally among the group. (Ayers, 2001, p. 14)

Each participant in this study could name at least one teacher who did, in fact, care for them well, a teacher who, in the words of Steve, understood that teaching is "*way* different than any other kind of job. You have to work with the kids, you know? You gotta give a little, take a little, give a little, give, take." A teacher who, in the words of Isabel, was "there to make sure if I didn't understand it, that I knew somebody else could help me understand it." Adel's description of an English teacher who was "actually there" as opposed to physically present represents an ideal that all young people are looking for:

> It didn't seem like she was just *there* to teach to get paid. It was that she wanted every one of her students to pass, and to *become something*, and like obviously she knew that it was my third year in English, and she made sure I was going to my English lab, made sure I was getting my work done, made sure I understood, gave me the time—if I did miss school—gave me the time to make up my work, and asked if I needed any help with it.

Steve's memories of another teacher willing to go the extra mile parallel Adel's description:

> She was so awesome! And she would work with you. She was one of the top ones that would work *with* you, you know what I mean? If you're failing, she will physically pull you out of a study hall, bring you to her class, and give you the test and say, "do this test right now!" You know what I mean?

Both of these teachers understood that the out-of-school lives of some young people get in the way of completing the mandatory tasks of schooling, and that adopting the rugged individualist position where each student is independently responsible for her academic progress—in spite of the unequal social and academic capital young people possess—dooms some students to failure (Currie, 2004).

Hannah and Cole both remembered teachers who treated them as equals and talked with them like friends. Of two teachers, Cole remarks,

> They were just cool. *They knew what was going on.* They were down to earth. They thought like you would think, and they'd just *use* it, and talk to you normally, not like a teacher, but talk to you like a friend.

Speaking about her favorite teacher, Hannah says,

> I remember one teacher I had. He could tell I was just, like, down. He was my favorite. And you know he asked me to stay after class, 'cause I had a study hall the next period, and you know, he just asked me, "Are you *okay*? What's going on? Do you want to talk about it?" And it's like, *wow*, you know, "*Thank you*!" So I told him all about it, and he told me if I ever needed to talk to him again, talk to him.

Cole's and Hannah's memories speak to teachers who respect students as full human beings and recognize the complex and often challenging out-of-school lives that their students confront. They understand, *without judgment*, that these challenges must and do take precedence over school requirements that appear, at best, remote in significance.

Theme Two: Being *Valued*

Make sure [teachers] don't favor the wealthy kids over people who don't have as much. (Hannah)

Teachers would have to have positive attitudes towards *all* kids, not just certain ones. (Adel)

I definitely would have the schools listen to the kids, not just certain kids, but *all* the kids, 'cause that was one of my biggest problems, going, trying to get help, and not being heard. (Iris)

Despite the claim that all children and youth should be treated the same in school, the reality is that some get more and others less, and paralleling wealth and income trends in the U.S., the children with the fewest needs typically get more care than those with the greatest. Evidence of unequal treatment is not lost on youth. Not only does it color their day-to-day interactions with teachers, it also shapes their self-perceptions, and their relationships with peers. Drawing on the scholarship of identity theory, Hodgson (2008) asserts that schools

operate as institutional complications to a biography of the self, by the ways constructions and discourses of students are unevenly distributed (Ball, 1999, p. 65). This becomes important in understanding how students interpret events as they occur within a "framework of hierarchy" (Pomeroy, 1999, p. 475) in which they often perceive themselves as belonging at the very bottom of a hierarchy of power, position, privilege, and respect. (p. 23)

Without being specifically asked, eight of the twelve young people in this study asserted that teachers like and support students who possess valued social or cultural capital such as wealth, family prestige, athletic talent, or normative intellectual skills. Mirroring the perceptions of dropouts in two other qualitative studies, these young people believed that "teachers had their favourites" (Lee & Breen, 2007, p. 338), and that they "were not as important to their school as the basketball players, straight-A students, or student council members" (Knesting, 2008, p. 9).

Isabel's description of a teacher who eagerly helped some students but ignored her repeated requests for assistance is heart-breaking—"It was pretty much like I felt I wasn't even there." Most of the young people in this study believed the "preps" and "jocks" were favored by their teachers. Hannah and Ivan attributed this favoritism to their greater economic resources, whereas Emily believed such treatment was given by teachers who identified more closely with these students. Of one such teacher, she says,

> He still wishes he was in high school, 'cause he was the popular jock type when he was in high school, and he favors those kids. [He] just jokes around with them more, pays more attention to them. That type of thing.

Adel believed that the kids who were the *easiest* to teach got better treatment (Fredricks, Blumenfeld, & Paris, 2004). Teachers liked best those kids who, in her words, "already knew what was going on, what the topic was about, [teachers] seemed to just really click with them ones, and the ones that didn't, [teachers] didn't really seem like they wanted to help them." Similarly, Emily felt that often, "teachers base their favorites on the students who do well in their classes, maybe the students who are funny or flattering to them or something more like that."

If favoritism is one reality, harsh treatment is another. Participants in this study who challenged school rules, or otherwise deviated from normative behavior, believed they received a disproportionate share of discipline. Ivan's and Hannah's experiences are consistent with Brown and Rodriquez's (2009) finding that "Students who try to assert their own will within school environments are often considered trouble-makers and punished" (p. 223). Jamie's and Steve's experiences with their principal support Lee and Breen's (2007) finding "that schools focus on particular academic and behavioural characteristics of students. When students do not meet these expectations, they are often explicitly excluded from education at their school" (p. 336).

According to several young people, the early impressions you create "stick," no matter how hard you try to recreate yourself. Hannah says, "Once you have your reputation someplace it's really hard to change it, so people knew me as like, you know, *bad kid.*" Echoing Hannah's assertion, Jamie explains how, in spite of his attempts to redefine himself, his previous reputation stuck and resulted in continuous surveillance by school staff:

> Alright, how do I put it? I sort of made an image for myself, couple years ago, like I was the *bad kid,* and I tried changing everything around once I got put on probation, and I already had the image, so the teachers still followed

me around, yelled at me about everything. I just didn't wanna be there anymore, just 'cause of all the nagging.

Capturing a sense of helplessness in relation to teachers who don't like you, Steve observes:

If the teacher dislikes you, sometimes there's nothing you can do, they won't even give you a shot. The teachers judge people, judge 'em like a book. Sometimes a kid walks in, say he looks like a quote unquote "scumbag," they won't even give the kid a shot, you know what I mean, and I've seen that happen all throughout high school. It's just messed up, 'cause that kid could be as good as anyone else. He might not have the income that the other kids have, but who knows, he could be just as smart, could be Einstein, could be anybody, you know what I mean. A lot of teachers pick their favorites from day one. They look at all their records, "okay this girl's smart, this guy's smart, I like these [students]." The first couple weeks they automatically know who they like and who they dislike, and from that point on, there's no ifs, ands, or buts. They like this person, they dislike this person, and couple'a times they disliked me, 'cause [of] stupid stuff, havin' the cell phone out, talkin', and just something stupid like that could screw your whole year up, you know what I mean, screw that whole class up.

Nearly all of the participants in this study classified individual school personnel as either "on my side," or "against me." Lessard et al. (2008) found that negative perceptions of student–teacher relationships was second only to grade retention as a predictor for dropping out (see also Rumberger, 1995, 2004). Fallis and Opotow (2003) discovered a relationship between class cutting and negative relationships with teachers, one that often had a *spillover* effect to other classes. This was the case with Adel and Iris, who confessed to missing even their favorite classes when those classes followed one taught by a teacher with whom they had a conflict. Leaving the building to cut the bad class, they did not return for the good.

Perceptions of favoritism and negative targeting not only affect the relationships between individual teachers and students, they powerfully shape peer dynamics within school. Emily's perception that the positive attention they receive "makes the athletes feel like they're better than other people," speaks to this dynamic (Heck & Mahoe, 2006). Ivan echoes this idea, focusing on how the resource of prestige shapes the preps' and jocks' identities and how those identities in turn promote exclusionary practices:

I think [the elite], what they see is that they are *revered*. They're put on such a pedestal by everyone around them, because they are good at: a) just having money, b) they're good at sports or whatever, sure, or c) they just derive their confidence from being the pretty girls and the hot guys. It's the ones who have money, and it's the ones who all kinda are able to draw their confidence up from these certain little traits about themselves and just section themselves off, away from everyone else. But it's always *above* everyone else, because everyone else seems to just revere them as these people who they all want to be. And they can sense that from everyone else, and they just, I believe, just hold themselves up there above everyone.

Socially constructed hierarchies such as these create a toxic atmosphere for peer relations and adolescent development, reflecting Noddings' (2005) claim that, "One of the school's most serious shortcomings is that it so consistently induces and maintains the creation of rivals and enemies" (p. 54). A culture that supports and values students unequally produces a *drama whirlpool* of competition and hostility between groups of peers, as described by Hannah. Similarly, Hodgson (2008) attributes the bullying that was so much a part of Isabel's everyday experience in school to "a culture of competitiveness and adversary" (p. 65). It is a culture that promotes the need for hyper-vigilance ("you gotta *always* watch your back," says Isabel), by producing extreme vulnerability and then failing to protect those most vulnerable. The result, according to Iris, is "Everyone just pretty much hitting upon everyone." From a narrow perspective, it is clearly better to be at the top of the hierarchy than the bottom. But as Iris senses, even the winners are losers when it comes to living in a world that is social. The energy required to "hit on" or to deflect the hits is substantial, stressful, and exhausting. Moreover, getting anywhere in life, from Iris's perspective, requires working *with* others. In the absence of cooperation, "you get nowhere."

Stratified peer groups may emerge in the absence of teachers actively playing favorites, but teachers reinforce these hierarchies when they repeatedly care for some students and neglect others, when they respond harshly to the behavior of one student, but turn a blind eye to a similar behavior in another. In contrast, teachers who mindfully value and affirm each student create a classroom that fundamentally challenges peer hierarchies and animosities. According to Sizer (1984), "teaching virtues like tolerance and generosity" is done, "largely by example or, better put, by the 'surround,' by the insistent influence of the institution [or teacher] living out those values" (p. 123).

Consider how three of the young people in this study talked about Mr. B., the "surround" he created in his classroom, and the values he expressed. Capturing the essence of *dialogue*, which is "improvisational and unrehearsed, and is undertaken with the serious intention of engaging others" (Ayers, 2001, p. 139; see also Carger, 2009; Freire 1970; Noddings, 2005),

David describes Mr. B. accordingly, "He let students speak their mind about the topic and all that, and then he spoke his mind about it. So we just kind of went back and forth and had nice conversations about it." Honoring students' ideas, Mr. B. often allowed the class to stray from the curriculum and wander unmapped terrain. David, a student who didn't shine on traditional academic tasks, experienced a rightful place on these open-ended journeys. Similarly, Isabel, struggling and invisible in most of her classes, says of Mr. B., "If I didn't understand something, he would help us explain what we got wrong, and he would joke around about it." Mr. B's classroom was characterized by what Sizer (1984) refers to as "unanxious expectation" (p. 174). He made it safe to make mistakes. In fact, he valued mistakes as a way to promote learning. Emily, a straight-A student who found traditional classroom learning easy, rarely encountered the humiliation David and Isabel had too often experienced. Yet her description of Mr. B. could have been made by any of his students who spoke with me:

> He had really good personal relationships with his students. Like he made *every* student feel like they were his *favorite* student. And he was always there to help people out, like when my locker used to get stuck all the time, I could go to his room and he would help me get it open. And if I ever had like any problems with my grade or something, I could always go to him and it wouldn't be awkward. He was really helpful.

Mr. B. valued all of his students: those who possessed normative academic capital and those who did not, the working poor and the middle class, the females and the males. To learn well, one must be engaged in the process, and to be engaged, one must possess a sense of *belonging*, of "being accepted, valued, included, and encouraged by others (teachers and peers) in the academic classroom setting and of feeling oneself to be an important part of the life and activity of the class" (Goodenow, 1993, p. 25). This does not mean treating everyone the *same*; it means honoring each and every student. In the words of Dennis Littky (2004), it means "treating everyone alike differently" (p. 73), or in the words of Emily, it means making "every student feel like they [are your] favorite."

Theme Three: Purpose

> *Why* do you want me to do this?
>
> What's it *worth?*
>
> What's the *use?*

Where is this *going?*

—Ivan

Nearly three-quarters of a century ago, John Dewey (1938) wrote:

> There is, I think, no point in the philosophy of progressive education which is sounder than its emphasis upon the importance of the participation of the learner in the formation of the purposes which direct his activities in the learning process, just as there is no defect in traditional education greater than its failure to secure the active co-operation of the pupil in construction of the purposes involved in his studying. (p. 67)

Although each young person who spoke with me could identify at least one teacher who cared well for them, and all experienced some classes that they genuinely enjoyed, none felt ownership in the construction of purpose shaping their school work. They perceived the highlights of their learning as random luck. What gives learning purpose? One aspect of purpose is a student's *intrinsic interest,* such as Henry's fascination with cultural studies and history. His Latin class captured both interests beautifully:

> [My teacher] taught you the language, but it wasn't trying to focus on the need to speak it 'cause it's not practical to speak Latin. So she wanted us more to learn how to read it. So we did a lot of Roman history and things like that and then we would get various scripts from that time, and then we would try and translate them. So I mean it was more like a cultural course, and it was definitely a lot of fun.

Similarly, Emily *loved* geometry. Doing proofs brought her joy. She would have welcomed the opportunity to continue studying geometry, but the state curriculum mandated a return to algebra and trigonometry, both of which she hated. Henry and Emily talk about the joy of learning something they loved, whereas Nathan's reflections on his chemistry class, where regular trips into the community were part of the curriculum, speak to a second aspect of purpose: the student's perception that their learning is *relevant,* that it has real-world use:

> I liked his class a lot, 'cause you'd *go* places, you'd *do* things. How you gonna learn about a sewage waste plant if you don't go there? That's what he did; he brought us there, instead of just opening up a book.

Relevance, richly defined and honored, extends well beyond the present moment. Students' common query, "Will this be on the test?" speaks to the impoverished and immediate relevance that has come to pass as instruction in classrooms across the country in the era of No Child Left Behind and Race to the Top. Deeply relevant learning, in contrast,

> should lead somewhere, in the eyes and mind of the student. This means that it must connect to wherever that student is rooted—his experience—and that it promise to take him toward an important place. It must be ultimately useful and patently interesting to him, at the time it is learned and in the future. (Sizer, 1984, p. 111)

Emily's description of an English teacher whose view of the world extended beyond the classroom captures this idea:

> She more wanted us to learn something in her class, and something that we would *take with us later on*, not a test grade that we would forget the next year. She talked a lot about different cultures, of different places around the country, and just tried to really enforce the fact that we aren't the center of the universe, and she really cared about that, that we would realize that.

It's difficult to distinguish curriculum from pedagogy, course from teacher, in many of these young people's narratives. Henry describes his Latin teacher as "one of the most genuinely nice people I've ever met." Similarly, the teacher who took Nathan to the sewage plant he describes this way:

> He got along with everybody. He was always there to help. And I liked how he would ask the students, "Can you guys have this done by this date?" We'd tell him if we think we could or we couldn't and he'd work with it. And if we couldn't, if we had something wrong, 'lot a teachers would just be like, "Oh, well, we don't care." But he would always be like, "Yeah, I'll extend the date for you, I mean I understand, stuff happens." So he'd always be there to help us out.

Emily's description of her geometry teacher hints again at Sizer's (1984) idea of unanxious expectation; this teacher refused to speed up in preparation for the mandatory state test: "He's really calm, he just puts everyone in kind of like a relaxed mood, so it's not all stressful if some students don't get it, and he has students in his room in his free periods *all the time*."

The enthusiasm Emily, Henry, and Nathan had for geometry, Latin, and chemistry respectively was most certainly enhanced by the quality of their teachers. Yet, excellent teachers are not enough in the absence of interest and a sense of relevance, as Henry's discussion of a wonderful math teacher—a teacher similarly praised by three other young people in this study—demonstrates:

> *Literally every day* if not every other day, Mr. R., the math teacher, was still like bothering me every day, even though he saw no response out of me. He'd be like, "You know if you need help at all, I'm here." I'm like, "Yeah, yeah, whatever," but it was still daily, I mean *he never gave up*. He spent that entire year trying to push me into like actually going through doing something.

Despite Mr. R.'s efforts, Henry failed the class. He simply could not understand why he was forced to take certain classes—"Like things I'm never going to use for the rest of my life, like math, essential to a point, and then after that, what am I going to use if for, ever? Unless I'm going to become an architect." In the absence of interest and a sense of relevance, Henry simply wasn't having it:

> If it wasn't interesting to me, then it might as well just not have existed. I would just have an apathy, and I would know I'm supposed to be doing this, but it was just kinda' "whatever." I should be doing *this*, but *that* is more fun, I'm gonna go do that instead, because I don't like this, I'm not interested in it.

David's general observation about the content and duration of schooling sums up the views of most of these young people: "I just didn't understand why we had to go for *so long* to learn that stuff when you don't really use that much of it in real life." The absence of purpose contributes mightily to the experience of boredom in school, so commonly identified by students (Bridgeland et al., 2008; Fallis & Opotow, 2003). This pervasive boredom, according to David, is intensified by repetition: "It's just the *same stuff* over and over again" (see also Gatto, 2002, 2009).

A key reason for this repetition is that everyone is required to learn the same thing, but interest in the material is remarkably uneven. Consequently, a student like Emily is denied the opportunity to study geometry in depth, while students like Ivan and Henry, who have no interest in proofs, must be forced to learn geometry's most basic functions. Henry fails, Ivan becomes increasingly alienated, and Emily is wistful. *Nobody wins.*

Not surprisingly, the primary reason that some of the young people gave for leaving school was that they genuinely felt that they had better things, more meaningful and useful things, to do elsewhere. This is consistent with Gallagher's (2002) findings:

The informants in this study maintained that they were withdrawing from something, but going to something else. Though possibly misguided, they perceived themselves as having acted constructively. In their thinking, they were leaving a dysfunctional, confused, unfamiliar setting and entering one over which they believed they had more control. (p. 43)

A similar perception is shared by Hannah and Henry:

I knew I wouldn't go to school, I wouldn't, you know. So I was like, it's really not worth it. So in my eyes, I did the better thing by not going back to school and just getting my GED. (Hannah)

Well, in my case, I was missing a single math credit that was going to prevent me from graduating [without having] to come back there and take half of a school day for half a year. Or, I could drop out and go to [community college]. It seems like a pretty easy choice there, start college early or wait a year and a half. (Henry)

Going farther still, several of the young people not only believed that they were leaving school in order to do something more constructive with their lives, they express the perception that remaining in school was holding them back. This, too, is consistent with the Australian early school leavers Hodgson (2008) interviewed, who felt that "the journey to complete year 12, or even year 11 for that matter, is too long and the personal costs too high compared with any benefits that may or may not be achieved" (p. 5). Nathan and Cole express this sentiment:

I'd rather be out working, making money, and get my GED. I already knew the basic stuff I needed to know, so that's what I was more into. I like to make money. I like to not waste my time sitting there learning more stuff that I don't really need to know, when I should be out making something of myself, making money, doing what I gotta get done to move out of my house and be happy by myself, on my own. (Nathan)

Well, I was offered a job in Oklahoma, hanging garage doors, making pretty good money. So that was pretty much the main decision that made me do it. I was already not going to school. I wasn't likin' it. So pretty much one of my friends called me one day and told me he moved out to Oklahoma and he's working for Overhead Door, can get me a job there, and I could move out of my house, and go out on my own, so I took advantage of it and I went and did it. (Cole)

For Nathan and Cole, schooling got in the way of their purpose of becoming independent. In Cole's case, the need for economic independence was not a choice; it was a necessity. He'd been more or less independent for years. Ivan's reflections are more existential, and suggest that schooling was eating away at his humanity, actually subtracting from who he was:

> You're learning this information so that you can pass your test either at the end of the month or the end of the week or the end of the year, but as soon as you're done with that, you don't retain it. *You* come out an *inch deep....The end result is nothing.*

Learning disconnected from purpose—interest, relevance, the future—is not only a waste of time, it can, according to Dewey (1938), rob the student of the desire to go on learning:

> What avail is it to win prescribed amounts of information about geography and history, to win ability to read and write, if in the process the individual *loses his own soul*: loses his appreciation of things worth while, of the values to which these things are relative; if he loses desire to apply what he has learned, and, above all loses the ability to extract meaning from his future experiences as they occur? (p. 49, emphasis added)

Theme Four: Freedom

> I just wanna—ah—hack at [high school] with a pick axe, you know. I just wish, I, I just [trails off]. Anything with such structured rules and structured requirements, I, ah, *freedom*, that's all, you know, *more freedom*. (Ivan)
>
> **Jeanne:** Alright, now if you think back to high school, was there anything you liked, anything you looked forward to during the day.
>
> **David:** I was looking forward to getting out of school.

Schooling is compulsory in this society; until the age of sixteen, children and youth are forced to attend or to be engaged in a state approved alternative. And, upon reaching the magic age of sixteen, if they choose to leave without completing their degree they pay a dear price. Like age-grades, separate subjects, and Carnegie Units, this coercion is an expression of the dominant common sense. Of course children and youth belong in school! And, of course, we need to force them to be there since many would choose other pursuits if given the option. And why is that? Perhaps, in part, because how we school children and youth contradicts one of our culture's most fiercely held values, freedom. My teacher, the late Frank Hearn (1985), captures the essence of this value accordingly:

> The individual is *human* only when *free* and free only when the sole propri-
> etor of his person and capacities. Accordingly, freedom requires the indi-
> vidual to be under no obligations except those incurred in relationships
> entered into voluntarily. We own ourselves, and in this ownership resides the
> right of individual liberty. (p. 11, emphasis added)

We justify the involuntary nature of schooling, in part, on the basis of
a phenomenon that appears natural but is in fact a social and historical
construction: adolescence. In *Act Your Age: A Cultural Construction of Adolescence* and *The Case Against Adolescence,* Nancy Lesko (2001) and Robert Epstein (2007) offer compelling critiques of this stage in the life cycle, noting
paradoxically that as the number of years to reach physiological maturation
has decreased, the number of years we compel young people to act like
children has increased. The historical construction of adolescence, they
argue, was more a response to the needs of organized labor, the professional interests of social scientists, and the world view of social reformers at
the turn of the last century than it was to the "real" or "natural" attributes
of teenagers. Likewise, educational historians have argued that the exten-
sion of compulsory schooling—in both years mandated and populations
served—has more often been a response to ruling class interests in social
control and assimilation than it has been in the interests of the students
themselves (Nasaw, 1979; Tyack & Hansot, 1982; Weir & Katznelson, 1988).

A final theme that emerged in this study was how overwhelmingly oppressive the young people experienced their confinement in school, and
how desperately they wanted to exercise control over their lives. How we
structure the school day, and as a consequence how we structure youth,
is profoundly disrespectful of their emerging need for autonomy. Emily's
observation captures beautifully this disrespect:

> It's so structured, like I mean it's not the same as it was in elementary school
> where teachers had to walk us in a line through the hallways, but it sort of
> is, because we get out for three minutes, like every 40 minutes. You can't
> get up and stretch, you can't do anything! You have to ask permission for
> everything, you can't even leave during lunch to go to your locker. It just
> feels like there's prison guards all around the school. It's like we're treated
> like criminals or something, not trusted at all. We can't go to the bathroom
> without having our passbooks and raising our hands in the middle of class,
> and then sometimes teachers say no to that too. Like we don't even have the
> right to use the bathroom.

Including Emily, eight of the twelve young people spoke explicitly to a
feeling of confinement; three others also used a prison analogy to describe
school:

[School is like] a minimum security penitentiary, [because] you're basically there from time to time, you have to follow every rule, you can't dress the way you wanna dress, there's so many codes. It's just that you don't have a lot of freedom over yourself while you're in school. (Cole)

School—is—like—prison. They *trap* you in there and they *force* you to do work! You're not allowed to leave, you're not allowed to do anything but what they tell you! You're under constant watch, and you're under constant just being told to do stuff. (Nathan)

The way that they kinda treat you is kinda like a prison. You're just, you're *trapped,* and they give you one choice, and if you don't want that choice, then "see ya," you know what I mean. (Steve)

David's observation gets at the heart of the matter—what students want or need at any given time counts for nothing: "Some of the teachers, like if you like had to use the restroom or do something really important, they wouldn't let you sign out—*no matter how important it was*—they made you wait till the end of the period."

Ivan critiques the lack of control he had over his body, on the one hand—"You're strapped to a one-piece desk"—and his mind, on the other:

They inject you with information, they're injecting you, into your head, information. It doesn't matter if you want to know it. It doesn't matter if it matters. It's just whatever the curriculum [dictates].

Henry's description of school speaks to a sense of simply doing time:

[School is like] work, in the sense that I had to get up at 6:30, and then I had to be there, sit there for however many hours, and most of the day I was in my own little world, like I just kinda fazed out, did what I had to do, and then that was about it. Outside of [a few engaging classes] it was just kinda like work, like drudge my way through it and get it over with.

Jamie says that school is like "the army [because] there's lots of rules and people are hard on you." Consistent with participants in Kortering and Braziel's study (1999), Jamie believed that most of the rules were stupid or pointless, creating unnecessary conflicts between students and staff: "I just didn't like how they nagged. They nagged about little [things], like rules that they shouldn't even worry about, like the hoods being up and stuff like that." One of these rules—no water bottles—emerged as a consequence of a few students using such bottles to smuggle alcohol into school. The practice of constructing general rules based upon exceptional behaviors is as common in our schools as it is destructive. In the chapter on social control in *Experience and Education*, Dewey (1938) speaks to this:

> There will be [students] who, because of previous experience, are bumptious and unruly and perhaps downright rebellious. But it is certain that the general principle of social control cannot be predicated on such cases. It is also true that no general rule can be laid down for dealing with such cases. The teacher has to deal with them individually. (p. 56)

Schooling, as we currently do it, denies students the construction of purpose as well as opportunities to exert their developing needs for independence and autonomy. And perhaps this might be more palatable if schooling did not embody such a powerful contradiction between childlike treatment and adult expectations. According to Hodgson (2008),

> Emerging adult identities can be thwarted and compromised by the culture and practices of the school. Students may be caught in a contradictory nexus. That is, an institution may expect adult behavior and responsibility from students but this may not be part of the institutional climate. (p. 61)

Trying to navigate this contradiction can be completely exhausting and feel hopelessly futile. Dropping out, in contrast, can be seen as an intentional act of purpose, an exercise in agency, as Ivan's story suggests:

> I feel like my education—my learning, me coming to myself, me growing and developing as a person, me learning about the world, viewpoints, religion, politics, sciences, everything like that—I started my education when I dropped out of school, because I was able to learn on my own terms and do things on my own terms, and I was not rebelling against anything. There was nothing to fight anymore, there was just me.

Reflections

I have a young friend named Maya. I've known her most of her life. She's now twenty and has just completed her second year of college. Maya has always been a model student. She's earned straight A's since kindergarten, played a sport each season, and was an active member in the student government and performance arts programs. She is in every respect, one of our school's "successes." In a conversation about my research awhile ago, Maya voiced her exasperation: "I just don't understand how *anyone* can drop out. School is *so easy!*" In one respect, Maya is absolutely right. For students who have achieved basic literacy and numeracy, and who can "attend" to instructions and follow rules, school *is* easy. This is especially true for students who, like Maya, come from homes of economic privilege, are fluent in the language of power, and have been socialized to normative school behavior. From an academic ability standpoint alone, eight of the twelve young people in this study could have completed high school without *any* difficulty, and the remaining four could have done so with individualized learning support (Bridgeland et al., 2008).

The bottom line is that U.S. schooling expects very little of *consequence* from its students, and is therefore "easy" when students are successfully socialized to expect nothing of consequence from their formal education. I've come to believe that the key difference between the dropouts in this study and school completers like Maya is less of aptitude, and more of willingness or ability to adapt to the structure of schooling. For a variety of reasons, completers adapt and dropouts do not. Through the common sense lens most people employ, this frames dropouts as lacking something: determination, intelligence, a willingness to "suck it up," or so on. Through a different common sense lens, it frames them as social agents in a fuller sense, and begs the question, "Is a decision to leave school always the irresponsible one it is often portrayed to be?" (Carger, 2009, p. 4).

I do not wish to romanticize the dropouts in this study. Each one confronts a multitude of obstacles in the absence of a traditional high school diploma, and all but two of them say they wish they had been able to persist, not because they now value what school had to teach them, but because they have encountered the brutal consequences of membership in this stigmatized group. Yet, from a purely existential perspective, all twelve possess sensibilities and real world skills that Maya lacks.

Moreover, when I reflect on the many conversations I've had with Maya over the years, her most powerful learning experiences—the things that "stick" with her to this day—occurred not in classrooms, but on athletic fields. Some of those experiences were directly related to improving her game, but others fall under Dewey's (1938) category of collateral learning— "the formation of enduring attitudes, of likes and dislikes....For these attitudes are fundamentally what count in the future. The most important attitude that can be formed is that of the desire to go on learning" (p. 48).

That Maya's athletics have been the source of her most powerful learning is no surprise, when you consider the total context. She has natural athletic talent and an incredible work ethic that is inspired by her passion for sports. She spends hours outside of formal practices working on her game, because she loves spending time that way. No one is forcing her. Maya has had her share of poor coaching and divided teams, but she's also had opportunities to develop her athletic talents within the best contexts. She's had coaches who view their players as evolving, and who see their own role as investing in their players' development over multiple years. Coaches who recognize the centrality of social relationships and interaction to the overall quality of the team. Coaches who understand that the full development of any one player is dependent on the full development of all. In many high schools, athletics are one of the only venues for the powerful learning experiences Dewey envisioned. Athletes are also valued within the stratification system of the school. A good athlete gets to do what she loves, and also gets lots of strokes for doing it.

But what about the rest of Maya's day—the parts that actually happened in the classroom? I can't say for sure, because it's been remarkably difficult to coax much information from her over the years, and when I have, it's often been of a negative sort—"I *hate The Scarlet Letter*! Why do we have to read this?" The absence of passion for what happened during the mandatory six hours of her day makes me sad. Once upon a time, Maya was a vibrantly imaginative, creative writer, and I wonder whether she is still inspired that way. Like my daughter, Paige, Maya was schooled in the TEES paragraph (topic, explain, example, summary). Did that kick the joy out of writing for her as well? Does Maya describe school as "so easy" because, unlike improving her game which has required intense practice and training, progressing academically has required far less from her, perhaps not much more than a willingness to follow rules and find "right" answers? After reading this chapter, Maya partially answered this question:

> One thing about athletics that has really stuck out in my head is that there is *always* room for improvement. This year, I sat the bench almost every single game of my first college lacrosse season. Even though it was really hard for me to do that, I needed it. On our days off, I would go to the field and do sprints and work on my shooting. In my preseason, I was at the field every single day working my ass off with my conditioning and stick skills. Even though it didn't seem to help much with my playing time, I *know* that one day I will benefit from all of my hard work and dedication. The difference between athletics and school is that once you earn your A, you are "done." You are *set*. You don't feel the need to really learn anymore. This is the problem with our school system. Even if I was a starter on the lacrosse team this year, I know I would still continue to push myself because it is my *passion*. (personal communication, May 31, 2011)

"Once you've earned your A, you are 'done.'" Multiple, interconnected insights are expressed by these eight words so poignantly strung together. Passion-based learning continues indefinitely. "Good enough" is consistently kicked to the curb by "could be better." Becoming a starter on the lacrosse team may be superficially comparable to the letter grade of "A," but Maya will never be *set* when it comes to her lacrosse skills. She'll work hard to become a starter, and then once a starter she'll continue to work hard, because as a starter the quality of her game will be even more important. Her drive is internal, and it is based on love.

Maya's observation also speaks to the impoverished reward structure inherent in how we school children and youth, and to the dispositions they develop as a consequence. Everything is externally constructed and imposed, from what the student will learn, to what constitutes excellent work. Within this context, the *symbol* of learning—the grade—becomes the only thing that matters, and once the grade has been assigned, the learning, superficial as it is, is over.

In reviewing what I had written about her, Maya agreed that she lacked many of the real world skills that the dropouts in this study possess. She believed, however, that she possessed several real world skills that they may lack. Significantly, these skills came not from the classroom, but, again, from sports. She writes,

> Being on some sort of athletic team for about ten years now has taught me a lot. Not only have I learned how to work with others effectively, but I've also learned how to put my team above myself and my own needs and wants. I believe this is a very important life lesson. I've also learned how to be a leader. I've learned how to lead by example; a lot of people can't lead in this way these days. But the most important lesson I believe I've learned, especially this year [when I had so little playing time], is how to continue to work for what I want, despite hardships. In life, there will always be obstacles that you need to overcome in order to achieve what you want to achieve. Through my athletics, I've learned to push through the hard times, knowing that there will be something really great coming for me. Hard work gets you places. (personal communication, June 1, 2011)

What if every young person's school experiences were modeled on the best of Maya's athletic experiences and supported the development of the life skills she identifies: cooperation, selflessness, purposeful modeling, persistence, and an agency fueled by a self-defined purpose?

I began this study wondering how we might better keep dropouts in school. Across these many conversations, over time, and with reflection, I have been repeatedly confronted with a different question, "Do I really think keeping dropouts in school is the answer?" If schooling remains as it is today, I think this answer is no, but I would extend this "no" to students like Maya as well.

In the final analysis, U.S. schooling defies rather than affirms multiple values we hold dear in this society: individuality, equality, purpose, and freedom. Successfully "doing school" requires students to become insensible to those same values, and to expect and accept nothing of consequence of their formal schooling. Through the stories of these twelve young people, I've come to agree with Gallagher's (2002) assertion that "school shepherds [need] to consider the strays when determining how best to tend the flock" (p. 36). Wanting to be known and valued, needing to act with purpose and autonomy—these are not the yearnings of "losers." They are human desires. Denying these desires is the price of high school graduation.

From this perspective, dropouts are like canaries in a coal mine (Singham, 1998). Once upon a time, canaries were brought into the mines because they were especially susceptible to carbon monoxide and methane gasses. When they stopped singing or died, the miners knew that these gasses had reached toxic levels, and the mine was evacuated. Similarly, dropouts are particularly sensitive to the school's multiple assaults on human desires and cherished values. Their withdrawal from schooling signifies an environment that is poisonously dehumanizing and alienating for all students. But instead of evacuating the schools, as we once did the mines, we ask how we can make dropouts hardier, less vulnerable to the toxins. Extending access to the high school diploma, as currently constructed, misses the fundamental needs of the flock as a whole. What is needed, for the canaries and the miners, the strays and the flock, is a rethinking of that diploma altogether. The one-size-fits-none, standardized program of study that promotes superficial learning, conformity, and obedience, and affirms only the narrowest of intellectual talents must be replaced with one that lovingly embraces and extends students' experiences, enriches their biographies, and celebrates and supports each of their talents and purposes with equal passion. We owe this to struggling students like Isabel and Iris and David, but we owe it to students like Maya as well.

10

Spin and Whisper

We live in a world of perspective and point of view, of meaning-making and interpretation, of narration and storytelling....Nothing speaks for itself.
—Ayers & Ayers, 2011, p. 81

The stories in this book and the meaning that these young people and I have made challenge the dominant narrative of schooling. According to the dominant narrative, "subjects and methods" and "facts and truths possess educational value in and of themselves" (Dewey, 1938, p. 46). In this narrative, learning is reduced to acquiring ready-made knowledge. In this narrative, teaching is reduced to impersonalized, standardized methods of knowledge delivery. In juxtaposition, our narrative reveals the student— Iris, Adel, Isabel, Ivan—at the center of the educational process, "a full human being, complex and dynamic, a three-dimensional creature with a heart, a spirit, an active meaning making mind, with hopes and aspirations that must be taken into account" (Ayers, 2001, p. 136). Our narrative denies that knowledge is knowable in advance, and separate from the student's biography and experiences. Our narrative insists, rather, that knowledge "emerges only through invention and re-invention, through the restless, impatient, continuing, hopeful inquiry [human beings] pursue in the

Canaries Reflect on the Mine, pages 105–118

world, with the world, and with each other" (Freire, 1970, p. 58). Our narrative is Adel's story of slow and gentle classrooms where students have *time* to make meaning together, classrooms where students' experiences and voices are honored for the powerful teaching and learning they produce.

Our narrative for teaching, then, is not one of methods of delivery, such as the mind-numbing TEES paragraph (topic sentence, explanatory sentence, example sentence, summary sentence) and the remediation lab. We seek instead a dynamic relationship, wide open to what may evolve in hopeful inquiry, animated by conversations that begin by "intentionally inquiring about the realities of students' lives" (Marquez-Zenkov, Harmon, van Lier, & Marquez-Zenkov, 2007, p. 410)—lives like Steve's, Hannah's, and Cole's. Our narrative for teaching obliges one to become fully "aware of the life stakes with which these young adults are literate," and to use this knowledge as a "starting point...to respond with practices and curricula that make school relevant to the lives of students" (Marquez-Zenkov et al., 2007, p. 408). The student-teacher relationship we seek is the journey Mr. B. takes his class on most days, a journey affirming each student's experiences and evolving knowledge. It is Mr. G.'s practice of being "actually there" instead of physically present, of "standing *right next to*" his students (Adel).

According to the dominant narrative, in which educational outcomes are pre-knowable abstractions, the assessment of learning and teaching is reduced to the ratio of correct to incorrect answers on a standardized test. Abel is not *sad*, he is *lonely*. In juxtaposition, our narrative reveals the futility of learning for the test. As Maya would say, "Once you earn your A...you are *done*." Or, in Ivan's words, "You don't retain it. You come out an inch deep. The end result is nothing." We assert that the value of an educational experience is a measure of how well it engages the student's capacities in the present and how richly it "prepare[s] a person for later experiences of a deeper and more expansive quality" (Dewey, 1938, p. 47). Ivan, the poet, needs words, but not a list of "expert" selected words to memorize. He needs, instead, the experience of searching for and even creating words that capture the meaning he wishes to convey. There is no standardized test for this. The meaning Ivan will create is his own.

The dominant narrative says that "choice" is the answer to failing schools. In this narrative, failure is defined hollowly as low standardized test performance, and choice is framed narrowly by a corporate model. We, too, see choice as the answer to failing schools, but we define failure as the denial of student purpose, a denial that has "the effect of arresting or distorting the growth of further experience" (Dewey, 1938, p. 25). Nathan experiences this failure as a socially constructed hatred of social studies. But he is poised to learn deeply as he imagines social studies of a different sort:

Instead of having social studies, having modern stuff, like automotive and how it's grown and how it's shaped the community. [Not] how to *fix* cars, [but] learn about past cars, what they did for the community and everything like that. Cars have been around [for a long time], so it'd pretty much cover anything.

The choice that we want is not between this charter school or that one in the educational marketplace, but rather the freedom to make mindful choices about passions to pursue and relationships to enter, and we believe these choices should be available to every student in every school.

Authors of the dominant narrative accuse ours of being utopian, too inefficient and expensive. Schooling flexible and personalized for each student? "Outrageous!" they assert. But they ignore the multiple inefficiencies and gratuitous costs inherent in the current system. Whereas sustained and sustaining relationships between teachers and students make purposeful and deep learning possible, we engage in the absurdly inefficient practice of assigning an entirely new cohort of students to each teacher, each year. Time that could be devoted to prolonged observation and conversation with each child, and to crafting pedagogical practices responsive to each one's needs, is denied in favor of a factory model of assembly where the teacher's job is to develop expertise with a discrete curriculum, rather than a deep understanding of each child or adolescent in her care. The far more effective use of human resources employed in looping grades and multiage classes—practices that are common in many countries enjoying remarkably high levels of achievement—are rare in U.S. schools, and have become rarer still in the high-stakes testing environment of No Child Left Behind and Race to the Top (Song, Spradlin, & Plucker, 2009).

In U.S. schools, we devote six-plus hours a day, 180 days a year, to the futile and demoralizing task of forcing pegs of all sizes and shapes into uniformly round holes. We create separate remedial labs for students like Iris and Isabel, who chafe against the edges, and then cruelly tell them that they are responsible for the resulting abrasions. We force Ivan and Henry to learn mathematical principles—superficially and fleetingly—that they have no interest in and can imagine no use for, while we simultaneously deny Emily the joy of developing a deep understanding of geometry, even though she would embrace the opportunity and learn with fervor. Embodying these practices of coercion and denial is the greatest and least calculable waste—the systematic squandering of the energies and passions of children and youth (Botstein, 1997; Epstein, 2007). Can we imagine a greater inefficiency than this?

And what about "costs"? Imagine the resources that would be freed up if the funds we now divert to the textbook and standardized test industry, and to highly paid "experts" who are hired to "develop" staff for better test results, were devoted instead to reduced class size and professional development aimed at reading kids and their needs. I say "imagine" because trying to determine the actual funds that go to corporate and personal profits is a remarkably daunting task. According to Foster (2011), however, both No Child Left Behind and Race to the Top are seen by many in the business world as offering remarkably lucrative profit opportunities:

> The education industry has naturally been a strong supporter of the new systems of high-stakes assessment and testing. In 2005 ThinkEquity Partners LLC published a report, *New Industry, New Schools, New Market: K–12 Education Industry Outlook, 2005,* for the Education Industry Association. It found that the education industry in 2005 represented "a domestic business opportunity in the [\$500 billion] K–12 market" of "\$75 billion, or 15 percent of all K–12 expenditures." As a result of the new standards, testing, and accountability measures of federal and state governments, plus the growth of charter schools, the K–12 education industry was expected to grow to \$163 billion (20 percent of the K–12 education market) within ten years. Already in 2005, K–12 purchases from the education industry included \$6.6 billion on infrastructure and hardware, \$8 billion on instructional content materials, and \$2 billion on assessment (testing systems). Spending on technology—overlapping among the above categories since software is incorporated in instructional content—was estimated at \$8.8 billion. The education industry report concluded that all of this reflected a much "deeper acceptance and integration of education and business." All sorts of "new money paths" were opening up.

Not only would such resources be better used to support intimate and personalized learning, redirecting our resources in this way could reduce overall costs, as the Finnish experience suggests. Although Finland ranks far ahead of the U.S. on the internationally renowned Program for International Student Assessment (PISA), its approach to educational reform is the antithesis of the model promoted in the U.S. (Sahlberg, 2011). Whereas the dominant reform model in the U.S. calls for more instructional time by starting children's academic training earlier, and extending the school day and the school year, in Finland, children do not begin school until the age of seven (Gamerman, 2008; Salhberg, 2011), enjoy 75-minutes of daily recess in elementary school (Abrams, 2011), and experience considerably fewer instructional hours overall (What accounts for Finland's high student achievement rate?, 2010). Between the ages of seven and 14, Finnish students receive roughly 5,500 instructional hours, compared to an estimated

7,500 for students in the U.S. (Salhberg, 2011, pp. 62–63). Moreover, the high scores Finnish students have achieved in reading, math, and science on the PISA, and the comparatively lower number of instructional hours they receive, have not come at the expense of study in "art, music, cooking, carpentry, metalwork, and textiles" (Abrams, 2011).

Furthermore, as part of on-going educational reform, Finland ended the practice of ability grouping in 1985 and has significantly reduced rates of retention (Sahlberg, 2011; see also Abrams, 2011). Coupled with these changes has been Finland's steadfast commitment to identifying learning challenges early and providing robust and holistic support in overcoming them (Salhberg, 2011). The social construction of "failures," "dummies," and "losers" so common at schools like Comprehensive High is virtually absent in Finland. Ethics of cooperation and community instead of competition and adversary shape student interaction in Finnish classrooms (Sahlberg, 2011). Students like Isabel and Iris are neither neglected nor held up to an arbitrary norm and found deficient.

Most importantly, standardized testing is minimal (Sahlberg, 2011). Teachers, rather than standardized tests, assess student learning. This reflects the extremely high levels of trust and professional autonomy (as well as competitive wages and high occupational status) that Finnish teachers enjoy; trust and autonomy that allow them to be truly responsive to the individual students in their classes (Sahlberg, 2011). Although Finland has a national curriculum, it is remarkably flexible; teacher autonomy, student choice, and local context shape how it is enacted (Sahlberg, 2011).

Finally, although "ninety-eight percent of the costs of education at all levels are covered by the government" (Darling-Hammond, 2010, p. 165; Sahlberg, 2011), Finland spends less on education than we do in the U.S. In 2007, Finland spent $7, 216 per student in elementary and secondary education compared to $10,768 in the U.S. (National Center for Education Statistics, 2007). As a percentage of GDP for the same year, Finland's expenditure was 5.6%, compared to 7.6% in the U.S. (Sahlberg, 2011, p. 5). In short, the Finnish narrative is not only consistent with the one these young people and I wish to advance, it demonstrates how a richer and more just story can be written with fewer resources overall when those resources are mindfully directed.

In *Finnish Lessons: What Can the World Learn from Educational Change in Finland?*, Salhberg (2011) credits many U.S. scholars, including John Dewey, for the remarkable progress the Finns have made in constructing a robust and meaningful school experience for all students. The desires so compellingly articulated by the youth in this study—to be known and valued, to act with purpose and autonomy—have a rich history in the social foundations scholarship of Dewey (1900/1990, 1916/1944, 1938), Friere (1970, 1998), and Greene (1988), to name just a few. The essential role of caring relationships between teachers and students as a vehicle for deep and relevant learning has been lovingly expressed by Noddings (2005), Ayers (2001), and Rose (1999). Models for such schooling are found, for instance, in the core principles of the Metropolitan Regional Career and Technical Center (Littky, 2004), the Coalition of Essential Schools (Coalition of Essential Schools, n.d.; see also Meier, 2002; Sizer, 1984, 1997a, 1997b) and, not surprisingly, in the mission and values of the institution where President Obama's children are formally schooled: Sidwell Friends School.

In spite of a long and deep history of alternative stories and practices, the dominant narrative of schooling has not only persisted in the U.S. (Tyack & Cuban, 1995; Tyack & Tobin, 1994), but has become ever more rigid and intrusive in classroom life. Beginning with the publication of *A Nation at Risk* (National Commission on Excellence in Education, 1983) and culminating in No Child Left Behind and Race to the Top, the last 30 years have witnessed an unrelenting neoliberal assault on public education, one that seeks ultimately to deliver it into the hands of the free market. The multiple "successes" of this movement are responsible for pushing struggling students like Isabel, David, and Iris out of school, for alienating academically strong students like Emily and Ivan, and for robbing "successful" students like Maya of an education that is meaningful and challenging.

Neoliberal interests have achieved these "successes" by masking the consequences of reform in a rhetoric of values, such as excellence and equity. But beneath the rhetoric a cacophony of contradictions abound. A socially conservative president wins support for No Child Left Behind by invoking the values of justice and equity. For the U.S. to make good on the promise of democracy, he says, we must challenge the "soft bigotry of low expectations" and "close the achievement gap" (Bush, 2004). Behind the lofty rhetoric, however, is a most stingy definition of equality. Bigotry is transcended, apparently, when all children are judged by the same tests and expected to perform at comparable levels, in spite of vastly unequal economic resources and fluency in the culture and language of power.

One administration later, a socially liberal president with a history of community activism adopts a capitalist metaphor for education that invokes the values of competition and winning. Rather than making a robust commitment to all schools and all children, recession starved states are given the opportunity to *compete* for nearly five billion dollars in Recovery Act money (U.S. Department of Education, 2009). Plans with a competitive advantage are those that agree to adopt a "common core" curriculum and national tests; link teacher evaluations to student test performance; expand statewide data systems; promote "innovation" by eliminating restrictions on the growth of charter schools; and "allow alternative routes to certification for teachers and principals, particularly routes that allow for [private and corporate] providers in addition to institutions of higher education" (U.S. Department of Education, 2009, p. 9).

The right leans to the rhetorical left and the left leans to the rhetorical right, but it's all in the spin after all. Under both the George W. Bush and Obama administrations, the rule of the day for *non-chartered* public schools, their students, and their teachers is rigid standardization of curriculum and instruction, test-based accountability with "teeth," and intrusive top-down regulation. Stunningly absent from both reform plans is Finland's commitment to equity *between* schools (Darling-Hammond, 2010; Sahlberg, 2011), where access to educational resources is framed as a human right rather than a spoil to the victors. Stunningly absent from both reform plans is Finland's parallel commitment to equity *outside* of school, where income and wealth differentials are meager compared to the U.S., and access to education and health care is universal (Lee, 2010). Finland's child poverty rate, for instance, is 3.4% compared to 21.7% in the U.S. (UNICEF, 2007, cited in Sahlberg, 2011, p. 69).

Juxtaposed to the spin is a dissonant *whisper*, an uneasy echo, expressed most often as a worried, insistent "But, wait . . . " Not fully conscious and not clearly defined, the whisper troubles the spin, like the prick of a slender thorn piercing the heel. Haughty with confidence, the spin asserts, "An equal education is a standardized education!" "But, wait," the whisper frets, "Each child is different. Each child's needs are different." "We will know good students (and teachers and schools) from bad, based on their standardized test scores," the spin promises. "But, wait," the whisper pesters, "What do the test scores neglect? What do they deny?" Where in the scores do we find Hannah and Steve's tenacity, Cole's self-reliance, Iris's grace, Isabel's kindness, or Ivan's uncommon ease with ambiguity?

As access to economic resources and political power contract, and as the effects of neoliberal educational reforms serve to marginalize ever greater numbers of students and teachers, the whisper is heard by an expanding number of people. Children and youth, always so much cannier than we acknowledge, know that we are wasting their time. Many of their teachers know it too. Parents who lack the economic resources to enroll their children in high quality private schools free from neoliberal mandates— and that is *most* parents—walk a tight-rope between their hopes for their children's educational success and their nagging sense that school neglects their children's promise. I talk endlessly about schooling with all sorts of people—my students, the many young people I know, their parents, public school teachers I'm friends with, the women at the YWCA where I work out, fellow patients in my dentist's office, shoppers in supermarket checkout lines, colleagues, and administrators. Whispers animate all of these conversations, and when asked themselves to imagine a better school system, these various people come up with many of the same ideas as progressive educational philosophers and the young people in this book.

The whisper offers a seed of hope. But in its current state, as my dear friend Darlene Gold so eloquently notes, it "is made up of wisps of individual energy that dissipate before it can gather and gain force or momentum." Reflecting, she continues, "I'm longing for a solution that stands up to the physics you've presented here. How do we attack, derail, redirect or dissipate the gigantic force of the spin?" (personal communication, June 8, 2011). Although the whisper intuits the dogged and knotty contradictions at the heart of the spin's cacophony, it is most often heard in solitude and experienced as a private trouble rather than a pervasive issue howling for public deliberation and action (Mills, 1959). What can our community— classroom teachers who daily witness the heartbreaking costs of the spin, foundations scholars who understand the contradictory impulses behind it—do to turn up the volume of the whisper so that individuals hear not only their own quiet yearnings, but those of their neighbors as well?

In the 1950s, a decade of rising incomes and a declining sense of community, C. Wright Mills (1959) characterized the main drift of U.S. society as one of unease, apathy, and indifference. As affluence and private consumption fed apathy and indifference, loss of community fed unease. Our time, in contrast, is one of declining incomes and deep economic insecurity. Apathy and indifference have been replaced by a paralyzing cynicism and a profound sense of hopelessness. Unease continues in heightened form, and today, as in the 1950s, it is fueled by social isolation and the absence of "publics"—spaces where individuals can leave their private orbits and come together to collectively analyze and act on the concerns they share.

If progressive intellectuals in collaboration with classroom teachers are to play a key role in the creation of such publics, we must cultivate a disposition to listen fully, to consider openly, to engage humbly, and to speak and question in a clear and unassuming voice. Our work, in the words of Freire (1970), must be "imbued with a profound trust in people and their creative power" (p. 62; see also Dewey, 1960). With them, we must collaboratively author and share stories that simultaneously reveal the dehumanizing consequences of dominant educational reform and the power of human beings to imagine and fight for something more just and democratic. The stories in this book so far have been about the lives and school experiences of high school dropouts on a rural, deindustrialized landscape. But they resonate widely, as I hope this final story, from the perspective of a teacher of young children on an urban landscape, will show.

"You are Welcome Here"

For over 25 years, my partner John has been a kindergarten, first grade, and second grade teacher in the same urban neighborhood; a neighborhood whose poverty rate has remained constant at 98%, while simultaneously deepening with each passing year. Knowing each child has been the foundation of his work; no child is invisible, no child is neglected. The mantra in his classroom—"We are all here to learn"—is not a cliché. It is a daily enactment. Like my high school English teacher, Lil Read, John's expectations for his students are extremely high, and he suffers no nonsense. But like Adel's science teacher, he sits right next to his students as they strive to meet the standards he sets. Based on both the authentic assessments he creates and most of the standardized tests he has been required to administer during his career, his students have consistently challenged the conventional wisdom that poor children can't learn. Nearly every student has made a minimum of one year's progress, and two or more years has been common, especially in the kindergarten-first grade multiage classes he taught for close to a decade before the testing mandates of No Child Left Behind ended this practice.

John brings stories of his students home every day. Two kinds of narratives have been especially common at our dinner table: joy-filled stories about kids discovering how smart they are and awe-filled stories of stubborn defiance. At the end of each tale of defiance, John's eyes will light up, and with reverence he'll remark, "That kid is *so* brilliant." From his perspective, it is not the child's job to curb her defiance; it is his job to engage and channel it.

John closely and continuously reads each child, qualitatively assessing where she's at in the present moment and what she needs to move ahead. He uses detailed running records of her reading, not standardized tests, to reveal her zone of proximal development and support her evolving literacy (Vygotsky, 1978, 1986). Consistent with Vygotsky's model of learning, John's ultimate goal is to advance each child's independence and efficacy. This is a very complex activity that both honors and reflects the multidimensionality of each student.

John's ability to locate a child's zone of proximal development, while necessary to good teaching, would by itself be insufficient. Added to this intellectual activity is his recognition that to engage a child in the classroom, he must also know and honor her context outside it. Striving to make personal connections with each child's family, his classroom is a public space open to all. To each parent or guardian, John says, "If you come to my room and the door is closed, walk on in. *You are welcome here.*" If, after the first couple of weeks of school, he has not yet met a child's parent or guardian, he'll walk the child home in order to make the connection there. He makes a variety of home visits each year, to share how a child is doing or to seek insights when a child is experiencing stress. He knows that his students' families are a resource, not an obstacle, to their learning, and his students' families recognize that he knows this. He regularly uses his cultural capital, such as his familiarity with the bureaucracy and its language, to help individual families advocate for their children. His relationships in the neighborhood are long term and extensive, as cousins, siblings, and even children of former students become current students. As he walks the neighborhood, students and family members stop him to say hello, or yell "Hey Mr. G!" from open windows.

John's relationship with James and his mom is illustrative. James entered second grade reading at a mid-kindergarten level. During the first week of school, John observed a significant gap between James's oral language skills and his reading skills. As a talker, James was lively and articulate. As a reader, he was unfocused and disengaged. John walked James home at the end of the week to have a conversation with his mother. Knowing John's reputation, James's mom received him warmly. Together, with James, they worked out a plan to communicate each day about how he was doing. James was given the important task of relaying communications back and forth. This was not framed as a punishment, but rather as a collective effort to help James learn.

As James's reading progressed, John suspected that he had a vision problem that had gone undetected in the annual school screening. As reading levels increase, text size decreases. Because John relies on detailed running records and continuous conversations with his students, James's inability to read known words in the smaller text stood out immediately. John went to the dollar store and bought James a pair of reading glasses to test his observation. When this worked, John contacted James's mom, who made an appointment with an optometrist. A less individualized assessment would have suggested that James should read below his actual level, rather than in his zone of proximal development.

Between the first week in September and the third week in June, James made two years of progress and was reading at a mid-second grade level. This achievement is a tribute to James, his mom, and John. It is a tribute to the small public they formed together, and it is in every way a model for what should be happening inside and outside of all of our classrooms. We would not need to talk about dropout prevention if it were.

Yet, according to the literacy assessment instrument John's district adopted in order to comply with the testing mandates of NCLB's Reading First Initiative, James's outstanding two-year progress is completely invisible. This instrument, called the Dynamic Indicators of Basic Early Literacy (DIBELS), is the antithesis of the comprehensive and balanced assessment engaged in by John, James, and his mom during the year. It also defies each of the desires that emerged from this study.

To assess "oral literacy," teachers are given a precise—teacher proof—script and a stop-watch. With the stop watch set for one minute, teachers count the number of words the student says correctly as she "reads" the DIBELS passage. Pausing, considering, and taking time to self-correct are penalized. In fact, if a student takes more than three seconds to self-correct, the teacher is instructed to tell her the word, mark it as incorrect, and, returning to the script, direct the student to move on. To assess "comprehension," teachers next administer the Retell Fluency part of the test. The script directs the teacher to say, *"Please tell me all about what you just read. Try to tell me everything you can. Begin"* (DIBELS Data System, n.d.). Again, using the stopwatch set for one minute, the teacher counts the number of words a student says as she "retells" what she read, yielding the "retell score." According to Shelton, Altwerger, and Jordan (2009), the retell score "is not subject to any qualitative analysis of content beyond detection of repetitions and off-topic comments" (p. 138). Speed and quantity—*not comprehension*—are the order of the day.

As with most standardized tests, students can be taught how to take the DIBELS, and with such preparation can raise their scores *in the short term*. However, those scores say nothing about the complex processes of literacy and learning. Moreover, teaching to such tests promotes student alienation *in the long term*. What appears as efficient from one perspective is remarkably wasteful and harmful from another. One does not need to be a reading expert to be skeptical of the alleged relationship between the speed and accuracy of oral reading on the one hand and comprehension and critical literacy on the other. Despite this, DIBELS has been adopted by schools receiving Reading First funding in 40 states nationwide (Manzo, 2005), including the district that serves as the background for this dropout study. According to Manzo (2005), the DIBELS has, in fact, "come to symbolize the standard for early-literacy assessment throughout much of the country" (p. 1). Given its patently vacuous approach to literacy, what explains its dominance as an assessment? Apparently in addition to the "efficiency" with which it can be administered, it also enjoys friends in high places. Two reports from the Office of the Inspector General (2006, 2007),

> revealed that Reading First officials and consultants with financial ties to DIBELS played key roles in biasing the [grant] approval process in favor of proposals that specified the adoption of DIBELS and that they contracted with consultants who financially profited from the implementation of the program. (Shelton, Altwerger, & Jordan, 2009, p. 138; see also Manzo, 2005)

According to the DIBELS assessment, because James entered and exited second grade "below level," his "at risk" status remains firmly in place in spite of the two years' progress he made. As such, John is a failing teacher. Because New York State "won" Race to the Top money, next year John's students' performance on tests like the DIBELS will be factored into his evaluation as a teacher. This is one reality behind the rhetoric of No Child Left Behind and Race to the Top.

Another reality is the systematic disruption of schools and communities as district administrators are pressured to "juke the stats" (Simon, Colesberry, & Kostroff-Noble, 2002–2008). For the first time in his career, John will be working in a different neighborhood next year, because his elementary school is being closed and reopened as a "new" middle school. In a bureaucratic sleight of hand encouraged in the high stakes testing climate, district officials managed to remove one elementary school with a history of underperformance and two currently underperforming middle schools from the data driven reform universe. The new school will enjoy a fresh start, free of a history of low performance. State regulators will be kept at bay for awhile longer.

The final six weeks of John's school year were bittersweet. He ruptured a disk in his spine in April, and just as our family responded to accommodate his injury, so did his students. The class bully took it upon herself to stand between John and anyone who looked like they were ready to jump on him (a fairly common event when his back is healthy). Children who were stubbornly defiant during the previous eight months became class leaders. Embodying the power of continuity of relationships (Noddings, 2005), at the end of each day during these six weeks, small groups of former students joined John to help pack up his room for the move to his new school. Juxtaposed to John's physical debilitation was the extraordinary competence and efficacy of these young people—qualities he, along with their families, had nurtured so well. They approached their work with intense purpose, carefully sorting and then crating thousands and thousands of authentic literature books according to reading level, author, and genre, pausing here and there to reflect on and talk about a remembered favorite. For John, these six weeks were filled in equal parts with sadness and love.

John's new school is as poor as the one he leaves, and I have no doubt that he will devote the remaining years of his career to the work of good teaching in this school and the work of cultivating relationships in the neighborhood that surrounds it. The visits to children's homes will begin in early September. He'll invite every family to visit the classroom, whenever they want. He'll give every family his cell phone number so that they can call him with any question or concern. He will do these things because he cannot do otherwise. These relationships, inside and outside the classroom, are what sustain him in his work. These relationships comprise the "home" he needs "to teach [and] act with thought and care and courage" (Ayers, 2001, p. 135). He will do this in spite of the spin. But make no mistake. The spin wounds him and his students, *wounds them deeply, every single day.* Imagine what they could do in its absence.

We have the spin to thank for bankrupt assessments that generate hefty profits for the few while denying to all students the close and loving assessment that each one deserves. We can thank the spin also for the disruption of continuity of people and place (Noddings, 2005), as scores of students and teachers—like John and James—are diverted to different schools and neighborhoods to make the stats look better. We can thank the spin also for falsely and cruelly labeling students like Iris and Isabel "deficient," and for prescribing standardized remediation labs for both even though their needs are not the same. We can thank the spin, too, for putting so much pressure on teachers to "cover" a uniform and arbitrary curriculum that they either do not see or feel compelled to ignore the out-of-school lives of students like Steve, Hannah, and Cole. We have the spin to thank for reducing learning to test scores and Carnegie Units, a reduction that robs students like Maya of a challenging education worthy of their passions and nurtures a disposition toward school learning expressed as getting an "A" and being *done.* And for young people like Emily and Ivan, who consciously refuse to participate in the dehumanizing experience of schooling, the spin offers the label of loser.

The spin has been authored by and for elites. It aims to reduce complexity, conceal injustice, and thwart deep thinking. In juxtaposition, the stories in this book—stories animated by insistent whispers—are rich in context, imbued with ambiguity, and unresolved. The story of James, his mother, and John, and the stories of young people like Isabel, Ivan, Maya, and Steve are *everywhere.* The ubiquity of such stories is a paradox of challenge and hope. The forces we are up against are pervasive, but our potential allies in the struggle for just and democratic schooling are likewise vast. Storytelling—by itself—cannot defeat the spin. We will have to fight fiercely, and the fight will be hard. But stories such as these show us that we're not alone. And stories such as these move us to seek the allies we need to wage a fierce fight. No, storytelling alone cannot defeat the spin. At the same time, the spin cannot be defeated in the absence of stories such as these.

References

Abrams, S. E. (2011, January 28). The children must play: What the U.S. could learn from Finland about educational reform. *The New Republic*. Retrieved from http://www.tnr.com/article/politics/82329/education-reform-Finland-US?page=0,1&id=PAkQ2h%2FiF5wiZTDtD1Hdr17Xg%2FtIxLOig5MOS7s%2Fc%20hExHO6auemmNrCMQ%2F%20Fi4s

Agee, J. & Evans, W. (2001). *Let us now praise famous men*. Boston, MA: Houghton Mifflin Company. (Original work published 1939)

Alliance for Excellent Education. (2009). *The high cost of high school dropouts: What the nation pays for inadequate high schools*. Washington, DC: Author. Retrieved from http://www.all4ed.org/files/HighCost.pdf

Anyon, J. (1980). Social class and the hidden curriculum of work. *Journal of Education, 162*(1), 67–92.

Ayers, W. (2001). *To teach: The journey of a teacher*. New York, NY: Teachers College Press.

Ayers, R. & Ayers, W. (2011). *Teaching the taboo: Courage and imagination in the classroom*. New York, NY: Teachers College Press.

Balfanz, R. & Legters, N. E. (2004). Locating the dropout crisis: Which high schools produce the nation's dropouts? In G. Orfield (Ed.), *Dropouts in America: Confronting the graduation rate crisis* (pp. 57–84). Cambridge, MA: Harvard Education Press.

Ball, S. (1999). New youth, new economies, new inequalities! Dimensions of diversity, lectures in the 1999 CIE distinguished visitors programme. *Center for Inclusive Education—Monograph Series No. 1*. Cottesloe, WA: Chalkface Press.

Bluestone, B. & Harrison, B. (1984). *The deindustrialization of America*. New York, NY: Basic Books.

Canaries Reflect on the Mine, pages 119–126
Copyright © 2012 by Information Age Publishing
All rights of reproduction in any form reserved.

Books, S. (1994). Social foundations in an age of triage. *Educational Foundations, 8*(4), 27–41.

Botstein, L. (1997). *Jefferson's children: Education and the promise of American culture.* New York, NY: Doubleday.

Bowles, S. & Gintis, H. (1977). *Schooling in capitalist America: Educational reform and the contradictions of economic life.* New York, NY: Basic Books.

Bridgeland, J. M., DiIulio, J. J., Streeter, R. T., & Mason, J. R. (2008). *The silent epidemic: Perspectives of high school dropouts.* Washington, DC: Civic Enterprises and Peter D. Hart Research Associates, for the Bill and Melinda Gates Foundation.

Brown, T. M. & Rodriquez, L. F. (2009). School and the co-construction of dropout. *International Journal of Qualitative Studies in Education, 22*(2), 221–241.

Bush, G. W. (2004, September 2). Acceptance speech to the Republican National Convention. *Washington Post.* Retrieved from http://www.washingtonpost.com/wp-dyn/articles/A57466-2004Sep2.html

Cameron, J. (1998). *Neither excellence nor equity: A case study of reform, reproduction, and resistance at an urban elementary school.* Unpublished doctoral dissertation. Binghamton University, Binghamton, NY.

Cameron, J. (2000). Social distribution, ghettoization, and educational triage: A Marxist analysis. *Social Foundations of Education, 14*(4), 19–34.

Cameron, J. (forthcoming). Autoethnography and the emergent public: Counterstories from a community college classroom. In E. A. Daniels & B. A. Porfilio (Eds.), *Dangerous counterstories in the corporate academy: Narrative for understanding, resistance, and community in the age of neoliberalism.* Charlotte, NC: Information Age Publishing.

Carger, C. L. (2009). *Dreams deferred: Dropping out and struggling forward.* Charlotte, NC: Information Age Publishing.

Chambliss, W. J. (1973). The saints and the roughnecks. *Society, 11*(1), 24–31.

Christenson, S. L., Sinclari, M. F., Lehr, C. A., & Godber, Y. (2001). Promoting successful school completion: Critical conceptual and methodological guidelines. *School Psychology Quarterly, 16*(4), 468–484.

Cisneros, S. (1991). *The house on Mango Street.* New York, NY: Vintage.

Coalition of Essential Schools. (n.d.). Retrieved from http://www.essentialschools.org

Currie, E. (2004). *The road to whatever: Middle class culture and the crisis of adolescence.* New York, NY: Metropolitan Books.

Dahl, R. (1980). *The Twits.* New York, NY: Scholastic.

Darling-Hammond, L. (2010). *The flat world and education: How America's commitment to equity will determine our future.* New York, NY: Teachers College Press.

Delpit, L. (1995). *Other people's children: Cultural conflict in the classroom.* New York, NY: The New Press.

Dewey, J. (1990). *The school and society.* Chicago, IL: University of Chicago Press. (Original work published 1900)

Dewey, J. (1944). *Democracy and education.* New York, NY: The Free Press. (Original work published 1916)

Dewey, J. (1938). *Experience and education.* New York, NY: Collier Books.

Dewey, J. (1960). *A common faith.* New Haven, CT: Yale University Press.

DIBELS Data System. University of Oregon Center on Teaching and Learning. Retrieved from https://dibels.uoregon.edu/measures/orf.php

Dynarski, M. & Gleason, P. (2002). How can we help? What we have learned from recent federal dropout prevention evaluations. *Journal of Education for Students Placed at Risk, 7*(1), 43–69.

Eaton, D. K, McKnight-Eily, L. R., Lowry, R., Perry, G. S., Presley-Cantrell, L., & Croft, J. B. (2010). Prevalence of insufficient, borderline, and optimal hours of sleep among high school students—United States, 2007. *Journal of Adolescent Health, 46*(4), 399–401.

Epstein, R. (2007). *The case against adolescence: Rediscovering the adult in every teen.* Sanger, CA: Quill Driver Books.

Erdrich, L. (2008). *The plague of doves.* New York, NY: Harper Collins Publishers.

Fallis, R. K. & Opotow, S. (2003). Are students failing school or are schools failing students? Class cutting in high school. *Journal of Social Issues, 59*(1), 103–119.

Finn, J. D. (1989). Withdrawing from school. *Review of Educational Research, 59*(2), 117–142.

Fischer, F. M., Radosevic-Vidacek, B., Koscec, A., Teixeria, L. R., Moreno, C. R. C., & Lowden, A. (2008). Internal and external time conflicts in adolescents: Sleep characteristics and interventions. *Mind, Brain, and Education, 2*(1), 17–23.

Foster, J. B. (2011). Education and the structural crisis of capital: The U.S. case. *Monthly Review: An Independent Socialist Magazine, 63*(03). Retrieved from http://monthlyreview.org/2011/07/01/education-and-the-structural-crisis-of-capital

Fredricks, J. A., Blumenfeld, P. C., & Paris, A. H. (2004). School engagement: Potential of the concept, state of the evidence. *Review of Educational Research, 74*(1), 59–100.

Freire, P. (1970). *Pedagogy of the oppressed.* New York, NY: Continuum.

Freire. P. (1998). *Pedagogy of freedom: Ethics, democracy, and civic courage.* New York, NY: Rowman & Littlefield Publishers, Inc.

Gallagher, C. J. (2002). Stories from the strays: What dropouts can teach us about school. *American Secondary Education, 30*(3), 36–60.

Gamerman, E. (2008, February 29). What makes Finnish kids so smart? *Wall Street Journal.* Retrieved from http://online.wsj.com/article/SB120425355065601997.html

Gatto, J. T. (2002). *Dumbing us down.* Gabriola Island, BC: New Society Publishers.

Gatto, J. T. (2009). *Weapons of mass instruction: A schoolteacher's journey through the dark world of compulsory schooling.* Gabriola Island, BC: New Society Publishers.

Georgios, M., Millrood, D. L., & Mateika, J. H. (2002). The impact of sleep on learning and behavior in adolescents. *Teachers College Record, 104*(4), 704–726 (EJ651404).

Giroux, H. A. (2003). Youth, higher education, and the crisis of public time: Educated hope and the possibility of a democratic future. *Social Identities, 9*(2), 141–168.

Glaser, B. & Strauss, A. (1967). *The discovery of grounded theory: Strategies for qualitative research.* Piscataway, NJ: Aldine Transaction.

Goodall, H. L., Jr. (2008). *Writing qualitative inquiry: Self, stories, and academic life.* Walnut Creek, CA: Left Coast Press.

Goodenow, C. (1993). Classroom belonging among early adolescent students: Relationships to motivation and achievement. *Journal of Early Adolescence, 13*(1), 21–43.

Greene, J. P. & Winters, M. A. (2002). Public high school graduation rates in the United States. The Manhattan Institute. Retrieved from http://www.manhattan-institute.org/html/cr_31.htm

Greene, M. (1988). *The dialectic of freedom.* New York: Teachers College Press.

Hearn, F. (1985). *Reason and freedom in sociological thought.* Boston, MA: Allen and Unwin.

Heck, R. H. & Mahoe, R. (2006). Student transition to high school and persistence: Highlighting the influences of social divisions and school contingencies. *American Journal of Education, 112*, 418–446.

Hodgson, D. (2008). *Understanding early school leaving: A narrative research approach.* Saarbruchen, Germany: VDM Verlag.

Hondo, C., Gardiner, M. E., & Sapien, Y. (2008). *Latino dropouts in rural America: Realities and possibilities.* Albany, NY: State University of New York Press.

Horowitz, I. L. (1963). *Power, politics, and people: The collected essays of C. Wright Mills.* New York, NY: Oxford University Press.

Jefferson, T. (1778). Preamble. In *A Bill for the More General Diffusion of Knowledge.* Retrieved from http://teachingamericanhistory.org/library/index.asp?document=408

Keene, E. O. & Zimmermann, S. (1997). *Mosaic of thought: Teaching comprehension in a reader's workshop.* Portsmouth, NH: Heinemann.

Knesting, K. (2008). Students at risk for school dropout: Supporting their persistence. *Preventing School Failure, 52*(4), 3–10.

Kortering, L. J. & Braziel, P. M. (1999). School dropout from the perspective of former students. *Remedial and Special Education, 20*(2), 78–83.

Lee, T. & Breen, L. (2007). Young people's perceptions and experiences of leaving high school early: An exploration. *Journal of Community and Applied Psychology, 17*, 329–346.

Lee, Y. (2010). Views on education and achievement: Finland's story of success and South Korea's story of decline. *KEDI Journal of Educational Policy*, 7(2), 379–401.

Lesko, N. (2001). *Act your age: A cultural construction of adolescence*. New York, NY: Routledge Falmer.

Lessard, A., Butler-Kisber, L., Fortin, L., Marcotte, D., Potvin, P., & Royer, E. (2008). Shades of disengagement: High school dropouts speak out. *Social Psychology of Education*, 11, 25–42.

Lincoln, Y. S. & Guba, E. G. (1985). *Naturalistic inquiry*. Newbury Park, CA: Sage.

Littky, D., with Grabelle, S. (2004). *The big picture: Education is everyone's business*. Alexandria, VA: Association for Supervision and Curriculum Development.

Losen, D. J. (2004). Graduation rate and accountability under the No Child Left Behind Act and the disparate impact on students of color. In G. Orfield (Ed.), *Dropouts in America: Confronting the graduation rate crisis* (pp. 41–56). Cambridge, MA: Harvard Education Press.

Manzo, K. K. (2005). National clout of DIBELS test draws scrutiny. *Education Week*, 25(5), 1–2.

Marquez-Zenkov, K., Harmon, J., van Lier, P., & Marquez-Zenkov, M. (2007). If they'll listen to us about life, we'll listen to them about school: Seeing city students' ideas about 'quality' teachers. *Educational Action Research*, 15(3), 403–415.

Mayan, M. J. (2009). *Essentials of qualitative inquiry*. Walnut Creek, CA: Left Coast Press.

Meier, D. (2002). *The power of their ideas: Lessons for America from a small school in Harlem*. Boston, MA: Beacon Press.

Michie, G. (2009). *Holler if you hear me*. New York, NY: Teachers College Press.

Mills, C. W. (1959). *The sociological imagination*. New York, NY: Oxford University Press.

Mills, K., Ed., with Mills, P. (2000). *C. Wright Mills: Letters and autobiographical writings*. Berkeley, CA: University of California Press.

Nasaw, D. (1979). *Schooled to order: A social history of public schooling in the United States*. New York, NY: Oxford University Press.

National Center for Education Statistics. (2007). The condition of education: Contexts of elementary and secondary education. Institute of Education Sciences. Retrieved from http://nces.ed.gov/programs/coe/tables/table-ifn-1.asp

National Commission on Excellence in Education. (1983). *A nation at risk: The imperative for educational reform*. The National Commission on Excellence in Education [Supt. of Docs., U.S. G.P.O. distributor]. Washington, DC: United States Department of Education.

Neill, A. S. (1992). *Summerhill school: A view of childhood*. New York, NY: St. Martins Press.

New York State Education Department. (2005–06). *The New York State district report card: Comprehensive information report.* Retrieved from https://reportcards.nysed.gov.

New York State Education Department. (2006–07). *The New York State district report card: Comprehensive information report.* Retrieved from https://report cards.nysed.gov.

New York State Education Department. (2007–08). *The New York State district report card: Comprehensive information report.* Retrieved from https://report cards.nysed.gov.

New York State Education Department. (2008–09). *The New York State district report card: Comprehensive information report.* Retrieved from https://report cards.nysed.gov.

New York State Education Department. (2009–10a). *The New York State district report card: Accountability and overview report.* Retrieved from https://reportcards.nysed.gov.

New York State Education Department. (2009–10b). *The New York State district report card: Comprehensive information report.* Retrieved from https://reportcards.nysed.gov.

Noddings, N. (2005). *The challenge to care in schools.* New York, NY: Teachers College Press.

Noguera, P. (2001). Finding safety where we least expect it: The role of social capital in preventing school violence. In R. J. Skiba & G. G. Noam (Eds.), *Zero tolerance: Can suspension and expulsion keep schools safe?* (pp. 202–218). San Francisco, CA: Jossey-Bass.

Office of the Inspector General—United States Department of Education. (2006). *The reading first program's grant application process—Final inspection report* (Publication ED-OIG/I13-F0017). Washington, DC: U.S. Government Printing Office.

Office of the Inspector General—United States Department of Education. (2007). *The department's administration of selected aspects of the reading first program—Final audit report* (Publication ED-OIG/A03G0006). Washington, DC: U.S. Government Printing Office.

Olson, K. (2009). *Wounded by school.* New York, NY: Teachers College Press.

Orfield, G. (2004). *Dropouts in America: Confronting the graduation rate crisis.* Cambridge, MA: Harvard Education Press.

Pomeroy, E. (1999). The teacher-student relationship in secondary school: Insights from excluded students. *British Journal of Sociology of Education, 20*(4), 465–482.

Randler, C. & Frech, D. (2009). Young people's time-of-day preferences affect their school performance. *Journal of Youth Studies, 12*(6), 653–667 (EJ865999).

Richmond, E. (2009). *Every student counts: The case for graduation rate accountability.* Washington, DC: Alliance for Excellent Education. Retrieved from http://www.all4ed.org/files/ESC_FedPolicyGRA.pdf

Rose, M. (1999). *Possible lives: The promise of public education in America.* New York, NY: Penguin.

Rubenstein, R. L. (1983). *The age of triage: Fear and hope in an overcrowded world.* Boston, MA: Beacon Press.

Rumberger, R. W. (1995). Dropping out of middle school: A multilevel analysis of students and schools. *American Educational Research Journal, 32,* 583–625.

Rumberger, R. W. (2004). Why students drop out of school. In G. Orfield (Ed.), *Dropouts in America: Confronting the graduation rate crisis* (pp. 131–155). Cambridge, MA: Harvard Education Press.

Sahlberg, P. (2011). *Finnish lessons: What can the world learn from educational change in Finand?* New York, NY: Teachers College Press.

Sennett, J. & Cobb, R. (1973). *The hidden injuries of class.* New York, NY: Vintage Books.

Shelton, N. R., Altwerger, B., & Jordan, N. (2009). Does DIBELS put reading first? *Literacy Research and Instruction, 48,* 137–148.

Simon, D., Colesberry, R. F., & Kostroff-Noble, N. (Executive Producers). (2002–2008). *The Wire* [Television series]. Baltimore, MD: HBO.

Singham, M. (1998, September). The canary in the mine: The achievement gap between black and white students. *Phi Delta Kappan, 80*(1), 9–15.

Sizer, T. (1984). *Horace's compromise: The dilemma of the American high school.* Boston, MA: Houghton Mifflin Company.

Sizer, T. (1997a). *Horace's school: Redesigning the American high school.* New York, NY: Mariner.

Sizer, T. (1997b). *Horace's hope: What works for the American high school.* New York, NY: Mariner.

Sjoberg, G., Vaughan, T. R., & Williams, N. (1984). Bureaucracy as a moral issue. *The Journal of Applied Behavioral Science, 20*(4), 441–453.

Song, R., Spradlin, T. E., & Plucker, J. A. (2009). The advantages and disadvantages of multiage classrooms in the era of NCLB accountability. *Center for Evaluation and Education Policy: Education Policy Brief, 7*(1), 1–8. Retrieved from http://www.indiana.edu/~ceep/projects/PDF/PB_V7N1_Winter_2009_EPB.pdf

Steig, W. (1976). *Abel's island.* New York, NY: Farrar Straus Giroux.

Summers, J. H. (Ed.). (2008). *The politics of truth: selected writings of C. Wright Mills.* New York, NY: Oxford University Press.

Swanson, C. B. (2004). Sketching a portrait of public high school graduation: Who graduates? Who Doesn't? In G. Orfield (Ed.), *Dropouts in America: Confronting the graduation rate crisis* (pp. 13–40). Cambridge, MA: Harvard Education Press.

Tucci, T. N. (2009). *Prioritizing the nation's dropout factories.* Washington, DC: Alliance for Excellent Education.

Tyack, D. & Cuban, L. (1995). *Tinkering toward utopia: A century of public school reform.* Cambridge, MA: Harvard University Press.

Tyack, D. & Hansot, E. (1982). *Managers of virtue: Public school leadership in America, 1820–1980*. New York, NY: Basic Books.

Tyack, D. & Tobin, W. (1994). The 'grammar' of schooling: Why has it been so hard to change? *American Educational Research Journal, 31*(3), 453–479.

UNICEF. (2007). *Child poverty in perspective: An overview of child well-being in rich countries.* Florence, Italy: Innocenti Research Centre Report Card 2007.

U.S. Census Bureau. *2005–2009 American community survey*. Washington, DC: Author. Retrieved from http://www.census.gov/acs/www/

U.S. Department of Education. (2009). *Race to the top executive summary*. Washington DC: Author. Retrieved from http://www2.ed.gov/programs/race-tothetop/executive-summary.pdf

Vygotsky, L. S. (1978). *Mind in society: The development of higher psychological processes*. Cambridge, MA: Harvard University Press.

Vygotsky, L. S. (1986). *Thought and language* (Rev. ed.). Cambridge, MA: MIT Press.

Weir, I. & Katznelson, M. (1988). *Schooling for all: Class, race, and the decline of the democratic ideal*. Berkeley, CA: University of California Press.

Weis, L. (1990). *Working class without work: High school students in a deindustrializing economy*. New York, NY: Routledge.

Weis, L. (2004). *Class reunion: The remaking of the American white working class*. New York, NY: Routledge.

What accounts for Finland's high student achievement rate? (2010, April 27). *Asia Society*. Retrieved from http://asiasociety.org/education/learning-world/what-accounts-finlands-high-student-achievement-rate

Wilson, W. J. (1996). *When work disappears*. New York, NY: Vintage.

Wolfson, A. R. & Carskadon, M. A. (2003). Understanding adolescents' sleep patterns and school performance: A critical appraisal. *Sleep Medicine Reviews, 7*(6), 491–506.

Wolfson, A. R. & Carskadon, M. A. (2005). Meeting teen sleep needs creatively. *Education Digest: Essential Readings Condensed for Quick Review, 71*(1), 47–51.

Yan, B. & Slagle, M. (2006). School start time and academic achievement: A literature review. Blue Valley School District Report Series. Available online: ERIC, ED493187.

Notes

Chapter 1

1. Pseudonyms have been assigned to all individuals who are not members of my family or colleagues of mine.
2. Pseudonym.
3. School completion rates are published each year for each district in the New York State Education Department's Comprehensive Information Reports (https://reportcards.nysed.gov). The higher than average dropout rate for Comprehensive Junior Senior High School was further confirmed by an internal study of the dropout rate: "Through various lines of communication that exist between district and state representatives as well as data that has been publicly released in the past two years [2005–06], it has been highlighted that [Comprehensive High School] has a higher-than-average dropout rate...between 15 percent and 20 percent of the annual graduating cohort, well above the state average for similar schools [and] our local data is more accurate than state reported data with a higher dropout rate reported locally (i.e., state reports dropout for 2000 cohort at 18 percent when, in reality, it is 23 percent)" (n.p.).
4. All demographic data are from the U.S. Census Bureau's *2005–2009 American Community Survey.*

Chapter 4

1. Because students are required to complete four Carnegie Units in English— or the equivalent of four full years of English Language Arts instruction— even one failure places students at risk for not graduating on time. According to Adel, her guidance counselor completely dropped the ball here. During

---

part of this exchange, I ask, "So that second year you were taking ninth grade English, would your grades have indicated to your guidance counselor that you were struggling?" She answers, "Yeah. I was failing, I was failing *horribly*. And actually, when I was in tenth grade and doing ninth grade English, my mom is the one at the end of the year, when [my guidance counselor] called us in, [my mom] is the one that said 'Well don't you think my daughter should be in an English lab?' And then the next year, I get my schedule and I have an English lab. And it's just, it's pretty sad that my mom's not there at the school and doesn't see my grades all the time, and where the guidance counselor, they have my grades, and they should've obviously seen that I need an English lab."

Chapter 7

1. I struggled mightily with how to best describe Iris's eyes, because they are really extraordinary. Finally, I asked her sister, who has known and loved her for years, to do it for me. She captures their beauty perfectly.

Chapter 8

1. Ivan's experiences with marijuana, while powerful, were not frequent. In reviewing his story, he was especially concerned that readers might give his experimental phase more weight than it deserves.